MW01235835

"Gettin' the Business"

A
Sales Professional's
Handbook

Stanley H. Van Etten
&
Stanley L. Van Etten

Library of Congress Cataloging-in-Publication Data:
      Application in Process

ISBN 0-9651044-0-0

10 9 8 7 6 5 4 3 2

Second Edition

DEDICATION:

To salespersons everywhere, whose hard
work and productivity continue to
provide business and industry with a
reason for being.

ABOUT THE AUTHORS

This book was written by a father-son author team. The son, Stanley H. Van Etten, is the President and CEO of Mayflower Holdings, Inc. The father, Stanley L. Van Etten, formerly with McGraw-Hill, Inc., is a professional writer.

Stanley H. Van Etten

Since graduating from Florida State University in 1984, Stan has raised over a billion dollars in investment capital in his career as an investment banker and venture capitalist. Recruited by a Wall Street brokerage firm after graduation, he joined the ranks of the company's 1200 brokers and in less than two years became the firm's top salesman. Courted by another Wall Street company in 1988 to head its North Carolina operations, Stan moved from Florida to Raleigh, North Carolina to take on the responsibilities of a Regional Vice President with his new firm. In just two years he lifted his regional office from a position of obscurity to the company's third most productive sales group.

Although still working full-time with the brokerage firm, in the fall of 1992 Stan (seeking to expand his professional horizons) enrolled in Duke University's "Evening Executive MBA Program." In January of 1993 he created his own company - Mayflower Holdings, Inc. - an investment banking consulting firm specializing in venture capital projects, corporate start-ups, and crisis management. As a professional consultant, Stan has worked with more than 50 "Fortune 500" companies, assisting them in the areas of sales, sales management, marketing, and investment banking. He is registered as a "Securities Principal" with the SEC and NASD. This present book had its genesis as a training manual which Stan wrote and published for his brokers. He later developed it further under the title Salesman's Road to use with his Professional Sales & Marketing Consulting Service.

Stan is married and lives with his wife, Kerry, in Raleigh, North Carolina. They have three young sons who love soccer and collecting small "critters" from the stream on their grandparents' farm. Stan enjoys golf, hunting and fishing, and most outdoor sports. He is also an avid chess player.

Stanley L. Van Etten

After earning two graduate degrees at the University of Chicago and completing doctoral course work in English at Auburn University, Stan launched his academic career in a state college in Florida where he served as a professor and department head until 1986 when he joined the College Division of McGraw-Hill, Inc. to do field editorial work and market college textbooks. In 1994 he achieved his long-held goal of becoming a full-time professional writer.

Writing is nothing new to Stan. As an English professor, he taught it for 18 years and wrote extensively on a wide variety of academic topics. As a college administrator, he frequently found himself writing about organizational and managerial problems and solutions. Then, going to work for a major publishing house, he found himself challenged with the demand for many new kinds of writing - sales manuals, marketing and editorial reports, manuscript tracking, promotional pieces, professional seminar presentations, etc.

Stan met the challenge! Editors, Marketing Managers, and Field Managers at McGraw-Hill praised his many editorial and marketing reports. Marketing Managers repeatedly requested him to write lengthy sales manuals (for important new-edition books) to serve as guides for the entire field sales force. He was selected for the prestigious "Marketing Reporter of the Year" award, and at annual company Sales Meetings was twice chosen as "Best All-Around Contributor."

Recently completing a series of articles on "The Language of Business" for a regional magazine, Stan is committed to several major writing projects which will extend into the new year. His dual background as an educator and sales rep provided him with just the right perspective for transforming (revising and expanding) his son's sales training manual (Salesman's Road) into this present book - "Gettin' the Business" A Sales Professional's Handbook.

Stan is married and lives with his wife, Deborah, on a farm in North Carolina, not far from the Blue Ridge Parkway. They have five grown sons and nine grandchildren. Stan is an American history buff, likes mountain hiking, collects railroadiana, and enjoys a good game of chess.

INTRODUCTION

This book is intended to be a stand-alone training manual for individuals who already are, or who are seeking to become, professional salespersons. Experienced salespeople will find many points and illustrations that will evoke involuntary, confirmatory head nodding (not of the sleeping variety); yet they will also find suggestions and analytical material that will provide new insights into, and understanding of, their chosen profession. Novices, on the other hand, will discover a wealth of practical "how to" information as well as an abundance of psychological and philosophical perspectives upon which they can build their burgeoning sales careers.

The book has the advantage of being the product of two authors who reflect not only generational differences but also generically different experiences in the real world of sales. The younger writer sold securities (stocks, bonds, etc.) in a marketplace that was infinitely large but extremely competitive. The older writer sold college textbooks in a finite market circumscribed by the boundaries of the traditional "sales territory" and crowded with "book reps" from competing publishers. Naturally then, the book is comprehensive in its coverage of both the "hard" and "soft" sell, though it has become next to impossible nowadays to come across cases where the two are not intertwined and overlapped.

The intention of the authors was to write a book that would be helpful to salespersons engaged in the most diverse types of sales. There are fundamental and universal strategies for selling that are relevant and productive regardless of the product or service being sold. It is upon these foundational insights that the authors have focused. But time-proven strategies and insights are never presented as mere theories in the abstract; they are always illustrated through real-world examples of the most concrete type.

This new second edition of *"Gettin' the Business"* features a 3-chapter *Appendix* on Network Marketing - an exploding industry that has more than 12 million sales representatives worldwide and which will do more than $30 billion in sales this year. Many companies are looking to network marketing as the vehicle which can provide them with dramatically increased sales production, and many individuals are joining the industry in order to radically increase their earning potential and, at the same time, put behind them their anxiety about job security.

The level of this book is practical, which is not to say that it is low. The authors are committed to the principle that there is no added value passed on to the reader by their using forty words where twenty would have sufficed. Also, it is the belief of the writers that a good straightforward writing style doesn't need to go out of its way to use "ten dollar" words where "fifty-cent" words would work just as well. In the case of word choice, bigger is not necessarily better. Good writing aims to instruct, not baffle.

Finally, the nature of the subject matter of this book required the unending use of certain words such as: prospect, customer, salesperson, etc. In order to avoid endless repetition of these words the writers chose to use the third-person pronouns *he, him, his*. They realized that by using these masculine pronouns without the alternative feminine counterparts, i.e., *he/she, him/her, and his/her,* they could be vulnerable to the charge of using sexist language. The authors strongly believe that language should be gender neutral whenever practical, but they felt that readers would grow weary of what would soon begin to feel like an almost infinite use of dual, slash-separated pronouns.

Readers of this book who wish to obtain additional copies at a reduced price direct from the publisher should contact the publisher's agent. See the final page of this book for detailed information regarding address and prices.

"Gettin' the Business"

A
Sales Professional's
Handbook

1

COMMUNICATION

Introduction

This book is about selling. You can't sell if you can't communicate. It's as simple as that. No matter how finely tuned your company's marketing strategy is, or how much it spends on advertising, salespersons still have to take their product or service to buyers. And that's where the rubber meets the road. If effective communication doesn't take place when sales rep meets prospect, then the game is off, called on account of poor and ineffective communication.

Flawed Communication

Communication always involves two things: the **sending** of a message and the **reception** of that message. Both elements have to be present for communication to occur. But the process is often flawed; it can break down at either end - the sending-end or the receiving-end.

SENDING A MESSAGE. If a person sends a message that is flawed, a message whose wording and/or punctuation obscures or distorts the intended meaning, the result is an unclear or misleading message. The example below, taken from an advertisement found in a business publication, is an illustration of an ambiguous message.

> *Example:* Servix Corp. is a workload management company. The cluster of services which we offer includes supplemental, functional, facility, transitional, and permanent placements. Call us to see how we can serve your business.

The message here is unclear. A quick reading of the ad leaves the reader up in the air as to what it is exactly that the company is offering to prospective customers. The phrase "workload management company" makes us think that Servix is a professional consulting firm. On the other hand, the phrase "supplemental...., transitional, and permanent placements" causes us to think that the company is a personnel agency which provides both temporary and permanent employees. Finally, we are left wondering if the words "functional" and "facility" mean anything at all, and if so, what. Thus we see how a flawed message can result in a breakdown of communication.

RECEIVING A MESSAGE. It's a bit more difficult to illustrate a breakdown at the receiving-end of the communication process. Of course we could point to the lines in the Servix ad above and say, "No reception here, since the message was unclear." But, in many cases, the responsibility for not receiving a message may rest entirely upon the receiver.

> *Example:* It is difficult to imagine the existence of even one school teacher who has not had a student say in response to a question stated in crystal clear language, "Would you please repeat the question?" Obviously the student did **not** receive the message, but the fault was not in the message or its sender. The problem was at the receiving-end of the communication process; the intended receiver was not listening.

CONCLUSION. And so we have seen the two most common causes for communication breakdown: (1) the failure of the sender to transmit a clear message, and (2) the failure of the receiver to listen carefully and effectively. But let's shift our focus now to **successful** communication. Let's look at what it is and how we can make it happen.

Successful Communication

Communication is sending a message and getting it received. As a salesperson, your main focus is on the sending-end of the communication process. You want to know how to construct and send a message that will be received accurately and positively by a prospect. The answer is simple to state, a bit more difficult to put into practice: Use the right words at the right time for the right purpose.

- Use the right words
- At the right time
- For the right purpose

We'll look at these three rules in more depth in a moment, but first let's set the stage for the kind of communication we're most interested in - **sales communication!**

Communicating in the Sales Interview

THE FOUR COMMUNICATION OBJECTIVES. Whether you are talking to a prospect on the phone or in person, there are four objectives that you must accomplish in order to conduct a successful sales presentation or interview:

1 - Get the prospect to **listen** to you.
2 - Get the prospect to **understand** you.
3 - Get the prospect to **accept** what you are saying.
4 - Get the prospect to **act** on what you are saying.

1 - GETTING THE PROSPECT TO LISTEN TO YOU. This is the **time** when you establish rapport with the prospect and get him to like you as an individual. The **purpose** of this stage of the sales interview is to get to know the prospect and see to it that he gets to know you. Of course we're not talking family intimacy here, but we are saying to talk about personal, non-business things - family, news items, weather, sporting events, hobbies, his office decor, etc. You want to establish a tone - a friendly, relaxed, trusting tone - at the very beginning of the sales interview. And the **words** you use at this stage should be warm, relaxed, friendly, casual, inquiring, interested, concerned, etc.

Far too often salespersons give short shrift to this stage of the sales interview. It is impossible to overstate how important this opening phase of communication with the prospect is. If a prospect senses that you view him or his company merely as a profitable sales target, there's very little chance that your sales message will get through, even if you present it skillfully and professionally. On the other hand, if a prospect feels that he knows you (even a little bit) and likes you, he will listen to your sales presentation with an open and receptive attitude; and what might have been a really tough sales call may turn out to be a lay-up (and very enjoyable besides) just because you accomplished this first stage of the sales interview so skillfully.

2 - GETTING THE PROSPECT TO UNDERSTAND WHAT YOU ARE SAYING. This is the **time** when you are conveying information to the prospect. At this second stage of the sales interview you are describing and explaining your product or service. The **purpose** here is inform the prospect in such a way as to get him to see the merit and value of what you are selling. You are appealing to his reason and intelligence. And so you should use **words** that are professional, informed, technical (without overdoing it), detailed, specific, logical, etc. This is the point at which you describe the features and benefits of your product and relate them to the business of the prospect. This is where you impress the prospect with the fact that you have done your homework, and done it well. And truth be told, if you accomplish this second stage skillfully, you're on the way to the bank!

3 - GETTING THE PROSPECT TO ACCEPT WHAT YOU ARE SAYING. The **time** for accomplishing this goal is all the way through your sales interview. The **purpose** of this objective is to encourage the prospect to believe what you are saying. You achieve this by being sensitive to him, by listening to his words and measuring his non-verbal body language. You take his opinions and questions seriously. You act toward him with sincerity, convincing him that you are concerned about the benefits that he will gain as a result of his doing business with you. The **words** that you use should establish your credentials for being honest, fair-minded, objective, professional, customer-oriented, and realistic. If you are successful at getting your prospect to accept your message, at the same time that he comes to understand it, you are only inches from the finish line of the sales interview.

4 - GETTING THE PROSPECT TO ACT ON WHAT YOU ARE SAYING. This is the **time** when you are closing the prospect. There is a sense in which the act of closing takes place throughout the entire sales interview, but it occurs decisively at the end of the meeting with the prospect. You established rapport at the beginning of the interview; you moved on to present and explain your product or service. You did everything you could to get the prospect to accept you and your message. Now your **purpose** is to get the prospect to act on what you have told him, to make the buy-decision.

Now you must bring together all of the motivation you have provided the prospect throughout the interview to a single, final focus, culminating in his saying "Yes" to your sales proposal. The **words** that you use here should be encouraging, assuring, supportive, confidence-giving, and congratulatory. The outcome of this fourth and final stage of the sales interview communication process should be exactly what you hoped for if you were successful in carrying out the three objectives that preceded it. Congratulations!

FURTHER ANALYSIS AND REVIEW. We must back up just a bit now and take a somewhat more flexible look at the four stages or objectives that have to be accomplished in order to communicate effectively in a sales interview. Let's list them again here in order to take a more informal look at them.

1 - Get the prospect to **listen** to you.
2 - Get the prospect to **understand** you.
3 - Get the prospect to **accept** what you are saying.
4 - Get the prospect to **act** on what you are saying.

In the explanation and analysis of these objectives (just completed above), we established something of a 1-2-3-4 sequence for accomplishing them. In the real world, of course, things don't always "go by the book." And that certainly is the case for sales interviews. So, the reality is that you are establishing rapport (trying to get the prospect to like you and **listen** to you) with your prospect **all** the way through your sales presentation, not just at "Stage 1." The same is true of the other three objectives. You are trying to get the prospect to **understand** you and the product or service that you are selling at many different points in the sales interview, not just at "Stage 2." The same logic applies to objectives #3 and #4.

So, what we are saying here is that flexibility becomes as important as formula. We're not going to forget about the four objectives that bring about effective communication in the sales interview, but we are going to stay open to our prospect's signals. The skillful salesperson understands that true communication takes place only when there is a genuine attempt to hear and to understand. It is crucial that you make the effort to know your prospect and where he is coming from personally and professionally. You need to be alert to his feelings about you and what you are selling.

As you gain experience in conducting sales interviews, you will develop an intuitive sense which will enable you to carry on a personal conversation with your prospect at the same time that you are proceeding with your sales presentation. You will have a sure feel for when to communicate on the personal level and when to communicate on the business level. This flow of communication from business to personal (and vice versa) should be controlled by the salesperson. The successful shaping of this flow will result in the establishment of the kind of solid rapport that leads to the prospect **accepting** and **acting** upon the message of the salesperson.

The Importance of Listening in the Sales Interview

TELLING IS ONLY ONE HALF OF COMMUNICATING. Earlier we defined communication as **sending a message and getting it received**. We want to turn now to examine the role that listening plays in this process. Many salespeople make the mistake of concentrating only on the message that they are going to send, and how they are going to send it. It does not occur to them that effective speaking (the delivery of their message) is only **part** of the communication process for which they are responsible. If selling involved only **telling**, what a simple job it would be! But, alas, it is so much more than that! Our telling must be tempered and moderated by what we **hear** from our prospect. We must be listeners as well as tellers. Selling is so much more than canning a single message and delivering it no matter what! When it comes to the message of a sales presentation, one size definitely does not fit all!

LISTENING IS THE OTHER HALF. Listening is about making sure that your prospect understands that you have a real desire to help him - to discover exactly what it is that he wants and needs, and then help him get it. Listening is about picking up on significant points that your prospect brings up, and making sure that he expresses them fully and clearly so that you understand precisely what he is looking for. Listening is about hearing what your prospect is saying so that you can shape your sales message in ways that will help your prospect see that your product or service fits the description of what he is seeking. Finally, listening is about hearing your prospect so that you can help him alter and modify the image of what he is looking for (assuming that it is similar to your product or service), so that it coincides with what you are selling.

Obviously, you must be a first-rate listener to accomplish the kind of listening we have just described. Most persons (including salespeople) are not first-rate listeners. We'll talk at length about how you can become one, but first let's take a look at the four categories that pretty well cover the waterfront when it comes to describing listener-types.

Four Types of Listeners

1 - THE "IS IT MY TURN YET?" LISTENER. This is the **non-listener**; he really does not hear anything that the speaker is saying. This is the guy who can barely keep his mouth shut until the prospect pauses for a breath, at which point he will cut him off and plunge into his canned sales pitch. This is the individual who, if he were only just a trifle less sensitive, would interrupt the prospect in mid-sentence and say, "All right, all right, would you pipe down so I can tell you about my product."

2 - THE "I HEAR YOU; I HEAR YOU" LISTENER. This is the **entry-level listener**. He hears words but makes no effort to get a message from them. He could probably repeat some of what he has heard, but no meaning has registered with him. He certainly will **not respond** to anything that has been said, nor will he rethink in any way what he is about to say, based on what the prospect has just said.

3 - THE "OH, SO THAT'S WHAT IT IS!" LISTENER.. This is the **fraternity-rush listener**. He is sufficiently focused on the speaker to get the gist of what is being said; but he is listening so that he can respond, **not** because he wants to understand. This is a high-risk listener because he is listening just enough to misconstrue what has been said when he responds. This could be the salesperson who, having just heard his prospect say, "And so down-sizing is something that we may have to do as a last resort," might respond by saying, "Oh, so you're wanting to down-size!"

4 - THE "I SEE WHAT YOU ARE SAYING" LISTENER. This is the **active listener**. He is genuinely focused on what the speaker is saying. He is listening in order to understand. This listener will not jump the gun by responding before the speaker has finished articulating his train of thought; and when he does respond, he will restate accurately what has just been said. This listener doesn't just **hear** what the other person is saying; he **sees** (understands) what is being said. Every salesperson should be this fourth type of listener - a skillful **active listener**. Now let's look at the steps that lead to becoming this kind of expert listener.

Non-Verbal Tasks That the Active Listener Must Perform

1 - LISTEN to your prospect **with the intention of understanding** him. Seek the meaning of what he is saying. Cut through any verbal fluff in order to see the core of his message. Don't be put off by any unusual or distracting mannerisms of speech. Don't lose track of what the prospect is saying just because you may disagree with it. Focus on one issue at a time, moving along with the speaker. Take notes to be certain that you don't miss something important. In order to better understand what the prospect is saying, think about how you would paraphrase in your own words what you are hearing.

2 - ACKNOWLEDGE (interiorly - in your own mind) the **prospect's views** even if you disagree with them. Don't let your opposing point of view keep you from understanding the other person's position. Don't allow personal preconceptions and value judgments to hinder you from fully understanding your prospect's point of view.

3 - RECOGNIZE the **tone** and **tempo** of your **prospect's speech**. There is a whole spectrum of possibilities here, and it is very important for you to understand what is revealed by tone and tempo. The range of moods reflected by tone and tempo runs from belligerent to self-effacing, from happy to morose, from judgmental to inquiring, from opinionated to reflective, from informed to indifferent, etc. As a person who wants to influence your prospect's intellectual and emotional posture, obviously you have much to gain by picking up on what is revealed by the tone and tempo of his speech.

4 - LOOK FOR NON-VERBAL SIGNALS GIVEN BY YOUR PROSPECT as he speaks. Body language is very revealing. Facial expressions, hand and arm gestures, leg movements, etc. sometimes say more than spoken words. A vast range of mental and emotional attitudes can be indicated by various non-verbal signs. It is important for you to discover quickly exactly where your prospect is located on a scale of possibilities that extends from confident to fearful, trusting to paranoid, stressed to relaxed, etc.

5 - USE POSITIVE BODY LANGUAGE YOURSELF TO ENCOURAGE THE PROSPECT TO OPEN UP. Effective use of positive and supportive body language on your part will cause the speaker to relax and give you more detailed information about his situation, thus providing you with valuable insights that will help you customize your sales presentation. The following practical suggestions indicate some of the things that can be done effectively in this area:

- Lean slightly forward in your chair to listen when your prospect is speaking.
- Look directly into the eyes of the speaker for brief periods of time when he is speaking. Don't look away every ten seconds, but don't stare so long at one stretch that he feels like he's getting the "third degree."

- Use a pen and legal pad to take notes when the prospect is talking. Don't make yourself look foolish by copying down everything he says, but write down important points so that you can reference them later on in your presentation. By taking notes, you make the prospect feel that he is being taken seriously.

- Nod your head from time to time to show that you understand the prospect's point. Try not to look like a clock pendulum that is swinging vertically instead of horizontally.

- Use facial expressions when appropriate; smile, laugh, frown, etc. in keeping with the context of the prospect's remarks.

- Use hand and body gestures as appropriate; index finger across chin, thumb vertical half-way back on lower jaw bone, chin resting on middle finger is a classic, contemplative pose. Try not to look like a comic version of Rodin's sculpture.

It goes, almost without saying, that there are **other** body language actions and habits which, because they are negative and distracting, should be **avoided** like the plague. Among them are such things as:

- Wiggling and squirming in your seat
- Sliding forward in your chair and lying shoulders back into a pre-nap posture
- Allowing the face and eyes to present a glazed or bored expression
- Coughing or clearing the throat frequently; sniffling your nose repeatedly
- Fidgeting with your hands or shuffling your feet

6 - DISCOVER UNDERLYING FEELINGS AND EMOTIONS. Try hard to get beneath the surface message that your prospect is communicating with words. Is there a whole different message that diverges from (or even runs counter to) what the prospect is saying at the surface level? Focus on the total mix of your prospect's communication process - his words, his tone and tempo, and his body language - to determine what he is **really** saying.

Verbal Tasks That the Active Listener Must Perform

1 - MATCH the **tone** and **tempo** of your prospect's speech. This does not mean that you should imitate or mimic the prospect; that would be ludicrous. It does mean that you should be sensitive to the manner of your prospect. If he speaks softly, it is probably a safe guess that he doesn't like boisterous speech. If your natural inclination is to crank up the volume level when you get excited about something, tone it down; hit the soft pedal! If your prospect enjoys speaking at a leisurely pace, go along with it; don't startle him with rapid-fire speech. If the prospect speaks at a brisk clip, don't frustrate him by droning along at a snail's pace. In short, do your best to match the tone and tempo of your prospect; you want his journey down Sales Pitch Road to be relaxed and pleasant.

2 - ACKNOWLEDGE (verbally - with spoken words) your **prospect's views**. Tell him that you understand the logic of his position, that you understand how he has arrived at his present point of view.

3 - RESTATE your **prospect's position** in your own words. This confirms in his mind that you really do understand where he is coming from. Refer to your notes and do a thorough job of restating his point of view. This act on your part will go a long way toward establishing a climate of mutual trust for the remainder of the sales interview.

Now, having gone to considerable lengths to describe the many things that you must do to become an **active** (expert) **listener**, let's call a "time out" and admit that in most real world sales situations neither the prospect nor the salesperson is operating out of angelic purity. In fact, from our perspective - the perspective of the sales rep - many prospects seem to have an inordinate ability to behave in extremely frustrating ways. That being the case, it becomes critical for the salesperson to avoid at all almost any cost (the ultimate cost being the loss of the sale) allowing a confrontation to develop between himself and the prospect. And thus we offer the following set of guidelines aimed at helping you to master the fine art of

Being a Non-Confrontational Listener During the Sales Interview

1 - FOCUS ON CLARIFYING VALID POINTS that your prospect raises **rather** than on defending an inaccurate accusation. Never speak in a defensive tone.

2 - FOCUS ON THE QUESTION OR ISSUE that your prospect raises **rather** than on the indictment that he has actually made. If he is attacking, answer his questions or concerns; don't attack his indictment.

3 - FOCUS ON UNDERSTANDING your prospect **rather** than judging him, even though that may be what he deserves.

4 - FOCUS ON THE PROBLEM the prospect is raising **rather** than on him as a person (perhaps a hostile person).

5 - FOCUS ON THE IMMEDIATE BEHAVIOR of your prospect, **rather** than on his overall (long-term) character.

6 - FOCUS ON INDIVIDUAL, SPECIFIC ISSUES RATHER than on the sweeping generalizations made by the prospect.

7 - FOCUS ON STATEMENTS made by the prospect that begin with "I" and respond to them with statements that begin with "You" **rather** than retorting with "I" statements of your own.

8 - FOCUS ON YOUR PROSPECT'S PERCEPTION and understanding of you **rather** than on who is winning or losing the "battle of words."

Using Different Types of Questions During the Sales Interview

Early on in this chapter we said that communication is sending a message and getting it received. Then we talked about how listening fits into the communication formula. Now we move on to deal with how questions fit into the communication mix. Questions are extremely important in the sales interview because they are the vehicle which enables both the prospect and the salesperson to gain critical information necessary for the transaction of business (buying - selling). So, let's look now at some of the most important kinds of questions that are likely to come into play during the sales interview.

1 - THE FACTUAL QUESTION. The purpose of this question is to gain factual information. This is a straightforward kind of question; there is nothing subtle about it. It probes directly for certain specified information. Often the factual question is structured in such a way that it begins with words such as the following: what, where, when, who, and how. Prospects are not usually put off by factual questions as long as they understand that the information being sought by the salesperson is relevant and necessary to the business at hand. In fact, prospects will very often have factual questions of their own which should be answered in a direct manner by the salesperson.

2 - THE EXPLANATORY QUESTION. This question is used to gain additional information or to broaden a specific discussion with a prospect. There are many points during a sales interview when either the prospect or the salesperson will want to obtain expanded information in order to better understand an issue being discussed. You can use questions structured like the following ones to do this kind of probing;

- "How would that help?"
- "How would you go about doing that?"
- "What other things should be considered?"

A prospect may very well ask you explanatory questions; when this occurs, you should understand that you need to expand upon a previous explanation(s) so that the prospect understands fully the point under discussion.

3 - THE JUSTIFYING QUESTION. The purpose of this question is to gain proof, challenge an idea, or get evidence to support a point. When a prospect argues an issue which you have doubts about, you should use the justifying question. If often takes the form of the following:

- "How do you know that?"
- "Why do you think that?"
- "What makes you say that?"
- "How is it that you are so sure of that?"

It is important to word this question in such a way as to require evidence and a detailed response. For example, look again at the last question above. Suppose the sales rep had asked simply, "Are you sure of that?" Then the prospect could have responded by simply saying, "Yes."

Sometimes a prospect will ask you a justifying question. When this happens, it is important that you understand that your own position is being challenged, and you should answer accordingly, giving specific evidence to support your point of view.

4 - THE LEADING QUESTION. This type of question is used to introduce a new thought or idea. It is a kind of "turning the corner" sort of question. It is used to move a discussion to a different focus or to a new level. Salespersons often use it to move a prospect toward a close, but it is also used to move away from a dead-end or negative topic. Leading questions sound like the following:

- "Could this be a possible solution?"
- "Let's see what you think of this plan?"

- "We both see the problem with that approach; what if we tried doing it this way?"

If your prospect uses a leading question, recognize it; understand that he wants to move the discussion in a new or different direction. Be sure to encourage his communication; you need to know at every point in the sales interview what your prospect is thinking and where he is coming from.

5 - THE HYPOTHETICAL QUESTION. This is the "What if" question. It deals with possibilities and probabilities. It deals with assumptions ("Let's assume that....") and suppositions ("Suppose that we could create a situation that..."). It is often called the "rainbow question" because it enables the salesperson to paint for the prospect a better, brighter world in which the return on his investment or the profitability of his company rises to a new level. Here are some examples of the hypothetical question:

- "If I could show you a way to cut your operating costs by 12 %, would you be interested?"
- "What if we could put together a plan that would allow you to retire three years earlier without diminishing the level of financial assets projected by your present program of investments?"
- "Can you imagine modifying your company's present operation in ways that would increase profitability by as much as 22%?"

On the other hand, a prospect may use the hypothetical question in a negative way, in which case it becomes (instead of a rainbow question) a kind of "doomsday question." Cynical, pessimistic, or cautious individuals are likely to make negative use of the hypothetical question. Here are some examples:

- "What if something goes wrong after my warranty has expired?"
- "But what if interest rates fall off? Wouldn't that be disastrous for this kind of investment?"
- "Suppose we can't find employees with the necessary training for the kind of expansion you're talking about."
- "What if I should incur major expenses as a result of a pre-existing condition before I've been in the program long enough to qualify for coverage of such a condition?"

Such negative hypothetical questions as these must be answered directly and head-on. Any attempt by the salesperson to evade them will only result in the creation of fear and doubt in the mind of the prospect.

6 - THE ALTERNATIVE QUESTION. From the standpoint of the salesperson, the alternative question is a "Win-Win" question. It is put to the prospect in such a way that he must choose one of only two (or a small number) of options; either (or any) option chosen is a win for the salesperson. It is a pushy question intended to intimidate in a subtle but acceptable way. Examples are:

- "Which one of these plans do you think is best?"
- "Do you prefer to meet again on Tuesday or Wednesday?"
- "So, do you want to order the two-door or four-door model?"
- "Will the $200,000.00 coverage be enough for now, or would you rather go with the $400,000.00 coverage to start with?"

Occasionally, a prospect will turn the alternative question on the salesperson. He may say something like, "Well, it looks to me like I'm stuck paying at both ends. I want the protection of the 'Extended Warranty,' but probably nothing will go wrong with my computer until after the warranty has expired; so most likely I'll end up paying for repairs anyway." Of course this is an example of the negative use of the alternative question. You can answer such a question effectively by pointing out a way to avoid at least one (or even both) of the negative outcomes conjured up by the prospect.

7 – THE COORDINATIVE QUESTION. The purpose of this question is to get the prospect to confirm a point of agreement or consent to a specified action. It might be called the "Amen Corner" question because, like the preacher who looks over to his staunchest supporters for vocal approval, the salesperson is counting on a sure-thing response when he asks the coordinative question. Here are some examples:

- "So, do you agree that this is our next step?"
- "Is this the proposal, then, that you want me to present to your Board of Directors?"
- "Will this schedule work for making the presentation to your department managers?"

Using Appropriate Words During the Sales Interview

Early in this chapter we defined communication as "sending a message and getting it received." We said that the successful sending of a message depends upon using "the right words at the right time for the right purpose." Now we want to look at words again - various kinds of words.

1 – AVOID WORDS THAT IRRITATE. As a salesperson, you want to avoid any habit or act that diminishes your ability to communicate effectively with your prospect. There are certain words and phrases that have, over time, been so overworked that most people are genuinely irritated when they have these trite and cliched words thrown at them (sometimes over and over again) in conversation. Listed below is a sampling of such phrases:

You know.	Understand?	Get the point?
See what I mean?	Got it?	You don't say!
Is that right!	But honestly now!	Really?
Don't you know.	I'll tell you what!	No way!
I'm gonna tell you the truth.	Now here's the deal.	Old buddy.

Any or all of these phrases may be real turn-offs for your prospects; so, be careful to avoid them (and others like them). What is bad about them is that (1) they smack of a kind of flippant insincerity or (2) they tread on a kind of familiarity with the prospect that does not exist.

2 - USE CARING WORDS. There are certain words that demonstrate your sensitivity to other people and to your prospect - words that show that you care about the person with whom you are communicating. Naturally, by using these words you enhance the quality and effectiveness of your communication. Here are some examples:

Congratulations!	I'm very sorry.	Thank you.
It was my fault.	I'm very happy for you.	Please.
You were very kind.	I beg your pardon.	Yes.
It was my pleasure!	Good for you!	You're right!

Sensitive, caring words help to elevate a conversation to a higher level. They reflect sincerity, openness, generosity, and perceptiveness. Used skillfully and sparingly enough to be credible, they aid the salesperson immeasurably.

3 - USE WORDS THAT PROBE. Throughout the sales interview, time and time again you will need more information from your prospect, an indication of where he stands on the issue under discussion, a clarification of a statement he has just made, etc. To obtain this information you must use probing words and phrases. Below are examples:

- I'm not certain I understand your point there.
- What is your opinion on this?
- Can you illustrate that?
- Will you help me here?
- What happens then?
- Why?
- Could you explain a bit further?
- How do you feel about that?

- What were the circumstances then?
- What are you looking for?
- What do you think?
- Do you have a projection?
- What will you need?

4 - USE WORDS THAT TRIGGER POSITIVE RESPONSES. To be sure, the saying, "Different strokes for different folks" applies to words as well as to lots of other things. But some words almost universally have positive connotations for most people. Much research has been done in this area over a long period of time, and a kind of consensus exists with regard to the positive-response value of many words. Listed below is a substantial sampling of these words. You should study them carefully and practice using them whenever they fit naturally into a sales interview. You should also add words to this list as you discover them in your day-to-day communication experience.

Affectionate	Ambition	Appetizing	Admired	Amusement
Bargain	Beauty	Current	Civic Pride	Clean
Courtesy	Choice	Durable	Dependable	Efficient
Elegant	Enormous	Economical	Earn	Expressive
Excel	Fun	Freedom	Fast	Faithful
Growth	Guaranteed	Genuine	Generous	Home
Happy	Honest	Hunting	Hospitality	High
Healthy	Independent	Justice	Kind	Low-Cost
Love	Lasting	Modern	Major	Meaningful
Necessary	Natural	New	Opportunity	Personal
Private	Proven	Progress	Pride	Prompt
Personality	Popular	Patriotism	Positive	Permanent
Quality	Relief	Reputation	Royalty	Recommended
Reliable	Real	Reward	Self	Scientific
Stimulating	Sociable	Stylish	Sympathy	Status
Sports	Strong	Safe	Significant	Successful
Secure	True	Tested	Tasteful	Time-Saving
Top	Thinking	Up-To-Date	Understanding	Volume
Value	Warmth	Worthwhile	Willing	Youth

It goes without saying that getting a positive response from the prospect is what sales is all about. So, every skillful salesperson will make it a point to use evocative words in order to enhance the communication climate of the sales interview.

5 - USE WORDS THAT INVITE ACTION. Several of the words listed above are words that solicit action on the part of the prospect, but as the sales interview draws to a close (pun intended), you should make a calculated effort to use words that virtually demand action. The words below are only a small sampling of the kind of words we are talking about here.

You	Your	Money	Satisfaction	Results
Save	New	Easy	Health	Love
Safety	Proven	Finalize	Discovery	Guarantee
Benefits	Realized	Started	Future	Control
Now	Decide	Happy	Yield	Determined

A single sentence illustrates the power of these words: "I **know** that **you** are going to be very **satisfied** with the **future benefits** that you will **realize** from the program **you**'ve **decided** on today.

6 – AVOID NEGATIVE WORDS. Any experienced salesperson knows that you can lose your credibility if you promise too much, if you throw around too much hyperbole. Fantasyland exaggeration should be left to small children and comedians. On the other hand, you'll never sell anything by accentuating the negative, by laying out doubts and ruminating about uncertainties. If a salesperson has doubts about the product or service he's selling, why in the world would a prospect want to take a chance on buying it. So, avoid negative and ambivalent words and phrases like the following:

I think so	I'm not sure	Maybe	Sometimes	I was wondering
I hope	Possibly	If we can	I feel like	Perhaps
Usually	Unless	At least	Until	For the present

Using an Appropriate Voice and Accent in the Sales Interview

USE YOUR OWN VOICE. Few people like to listen to a person who is struggling to sound like someone he is not! Phony accents and affected ways of speaking usually stick out like a sore thumb. A person who grew up in Atlanta will not likely ever speak with the same tone and accent as an individual who grew up in Boston, and vice versa. (And what a **dull** world it would be if everyone **did** speak with the same voice!) But this is not to say that anyone can afford to be lazy and careless about his manner of speaking. You need to remember several "Do's" and "Don'ts" with regard to your speaking voice.

Things to **do** when speaking:

- Speak clearly. Enunciate syllables crisply and cleanly.
- Speak with a pleasant tone of voice. Not too high; not too low. Not always the same.
- Speak at a comfortable pace. Not too fast; not too slow.

- Speak with inflection. Make sure that a question sounds like a question and that a statement of fact sounds like a statement of fact. Give more emphasis to words and phrases that are important, less emphasis to words and phrases that are not.
- Speak loudly enough to be heard easily. Not too loud; not to soft.

Things to **avoid** when speaking:

- Don't mumble words. Don't drop off first and last syllables of words. Don't treat letters that should be pronounced distinctly as if they were "silent" letters.
- Don't speak in a monotone.
- Don't speak at breakneck speed or at a snail's pace.
- Don't speak without emphasis (inflection). Your listener should be able to tell from your voice which points are important, and which are not.
- Don't speak so quietly that you are not heard. Your listener should not have to ask you to repeat things.

Relative to the final point stated above is this story about a junior high school drama coach who once admonished a group of young actors for whom he held little, if any, hope by saying,

> "I don't care if you're in the wrong place at the wrong time; I don't care if you say the wrong lines; I don't care if you look at the wrong person when you speak (etc., etc.); but when you do speak, you had better speak loudly enough for anyone sitting in the back row to hear you without even the slightest difficulty. Being heard is the **least** that you can accomplish. **Not being heard is unforgivable!**"

It goes without saying that the salesperson who is not heard by the prospect in the sales interview had better give it up and start looking immediately for another career.

Communicating With An Irate Customer

IMPORTANCE OF THIS TYPE COMMUNICATION. Learning to communicate effectively with an upset customer is a tough assignment. However, it is an assignment well worth mastering, for at one and the same time you are able to (1) solve a customer problem and (2) create a strong, long-term customer relationship. On the other hand, if you fail to handle an irate customer satisfactorily, you will probably (1) lose a sale and a customer and (2) lose numerous other potential customers as well. (On average, a dissatisfied customer tells ten other people about his problem.)

BE AN ACTIVE LISTENER. The best way to handle an irate customer is to do a lot of active listening. Let him talk; let him air his frustrations; venting them should, by that very act, provide him with some relief. Give him a sympathetic ear and have an open mind to his problem. Remember that this particular problem is of primary importance to him at this moment in time. Here are some specific things you should do:

- Try to **hear** the problem and **understand** it.
- Listen for **facts** and **feelings**.
- **Interject** with **reassuring words** without necessarily falling into a sympathizing mode.
- **Avoid** a **confrontation** or judgment of him as a person (or of his character).
- **Ask** a lot of **questions** using fact-finding words like **why, when, where, which, and what**."
  This provides positive feedback for the customer, demonstrating that you have a real interest in solving his problem.

PROMISE AN EARLY SOLUTION. After you have taken in all of the information that you can gather from the customer, tell him that you will analyze and evaluate it and get back to him with a solution within twenty-four hours. Even if your solution turns out to be a recommendation to stay with things the way they are (giving the prospect specific reasons for your recommendation), it is absolutely critical that you **do** get back to him within the time frame promised.

Practicing Communication

Every salesperson has plenty of opportunity to develop his communication skills in the everyday world of real sales contacts. The obvious downside of practicing your communication skills (or lack thereof) in the real world is that you stand to lose business if you make mistakes. So, it goes without saying that there is great advantage to practicing your communication techniques in an immune environment - that is, at home or with friends, or anywhere where there is nothing to be lost by your fumbling or stumbling.

WHAT SHOULD YOU PRACTICE? You should practice the two elements that make up the communication process - **speaking** and **listening**, sending a message and receiving a message.

HOW SHOULD YOU PRACTICE? You should practice by **seeing** how you speak and listen and by **hearing** how you speak and listen. You can **see** how you communicate by practicing in front of a mirror and by recording yourself on a video recorder. You can **hear** how you communicate by using video and/or audio recorders. You can practice alone or with another person or persons. In either case you should play back all recordings that you make and analyze them carefully, making written notes to yourself about strengths and weaknesses that you discover while viewing and listening to the playback of the tapes. When it comes to communicating, the old saying, "Practice makes perfect" applies. But it's **not blind** or **deaf practice** that counts; it's **perceptive practice** that makes a difference. Don't fall victim to just practicing the same old mistakes over and over again. Practice in order to **discover** your mistakes so that you can fix them, as in **get rid** of them!

And remember as you practice that you are developing and improving the most important skills a salesperson can have - communication skills. Everything else in sales hinges on your ability to communicate effectively because, as the old pros in sales love to remind us, if you're not communicating, you're not selling!

Summary

The ability to communicate at a very sophisticated and high level is one of the things that separates human beings from the world's other creatures. In the sales arena, communication skill separates winners from losers, successful producers from also-rans.

In this chapter we have tried to demonstrate that communication is not something that one person can *do* to another person. Communication is a two-way street; it can never be accomplished by the individual who sets out to do it *to* another person. Communication never occurs if the *other* person remains passive, indifferent, or antagonistic. The individual who seeks to communicate must *engage* the other person, must arouse his interest, must trigger an emotional or intellectual response.

There are many ways to describe the two-way street which is the communication process. It is telling and listening, sending and receiving, saying and hearing. The teller must see to it that his listener is *really* listening, and in turn must himself be a skillful listener when the other person responds. The successful communicator understands that you can't play ping-pong by yourself

Successful salespersons *like* communication. They understand that it is both a science and an art. There is more to it than *knowing* how to do it; one must also have a *feeling* for how to do it. Top salespeople constantly analyze their communication with prospects and customers. Every sales interview provides them with new "lab data" to study and learn from. They are communication aficionados, devotees, enthusiasts. They pride themselves as being individuals who have been initiated into the mystique of communication's inner sanctum. They know that their highly developed communication skills translate into *power*.

The elite communicators among sales professionals have mastered the training formula of "the right words at the right time for the right purpose." They have internalized it; it has become second-nature for them. They do it automatically in every sales interview. They have become like the big league pitching ace; they read their prospect perfectly and pitch to him with confidence and precision. To take the analogy further, they know

- When to pause and go for the resin
- When to toe the rubber and when to look to first
- When to eye the ump
- When to look to the catcher and shake off a sign
- When to stretch and when to deliver
- When to throw the high hard one and when to throw the change-up

Like the best pitchers in the big leagues, the best communicators in the sales profession know that they will occasionally have a bad day, throw some bad pitches. But they *also* know that they possess the *power*. They will pitch again one day soon, and they will win; for they are communication professionals. They have the requisite tools. To say it with baseball talk, "They've got great control and the 100 mile-an-hour fastball!"

2

TELEPHONE PERFORMANCE

Introduction

THE TELEPHONE AND SELLING. Many salespersons today are engaged in full-time telemarketing. All of their selling is done on the phone. They never see prospects or customers face-to-face. For these salespeople the telephone is not just important; it is vital! Many other salespersons use the telephone extensively to prospect, sell, set appointments, and confirm sales. Many businesses have an "800" number for customers who want to place phone orders or respond to advertisements.

Everyone in sales today knows how important the telephone is. The surprising thing is that many salespeople take telephone skills for granted. "After all," they say, "selling is selling, whether in person or on the phone, right?" Wrong! Professional use of the telephone for the purpose of selling is an acquired skill, a learned art. It is not like breathing; it is not something that "just comes naturally." In this chapter we will develop and describe the profile of the successful telephone marketer.

Voice

There's an old saying: "Seeing is believing." Well, your prospect can't **see** you when you're talking on the phone. So, it's what he **hears** that counts. And, of course, it's your voice that he hears. We mentioned some important things about voice in the previous chapter, but we will review them here in the context of telemarketing.

CLARITY. If you don't speak clearly on the phone, you're dead. You can't hand the prospect a flyer or brochure to look at. You can't give your words an assist by using body language. You can't drive home a point with a facial expression. You have to speak clearly so that your words are instantly understood and their message received by the prospect. Nothing is more irritating than attempting to listen to someone whose words are impossible to understand. There are **"Four Fatal Flaws"** that cause a person's words not to be understood: (1) mumbling, (2) speaking too softly, (3) talking too fast, and (4) speaking without (or with the wrong) inflection. Avoid these four faults like the plague!

PITCH OR TONE. An effective telephone voice ranges widely in pitch - up and down and in between - but avoids extremes. A mid-range tone is best for most conversation. A high or shrill pitch hurts the ears. A tone that is too low sounds melodramatic. A nasal twang sounds uncultivated. A gravelly voice sounds like phlegm in the throat and is irritating. An unvaried single pitch - a monotone - is an invitation to the prospect to hang up.

VOLUME. No one likes to be shouted at, and no one wants to have to strain to hear what someone else is saying. Speak loudly enough to be easily heard, but softly enough not to be offensive. A skillful speaker varies the volume of his voice for dramatic effect and points of emphasis. Interestingly, the volume is often lowered to make very important points.

EXPRESSION AND INFLECTION. The expression or inflection that a person uses gives his voice personality and character. Inflection is what we do to words and phrases to make them say something extra - something more than just the sum total of their combined dictionary definitions. Inflection may punch a word harder in order to give it special meaning, may take a word or phrase up or down the scale of pitch, may stretch a syllable within a word. It can do any number of things to make speech more appealing and enhance the meaning that it communicates. Many people define inflection by saying what it is **not**. It is not speaking in a monotone.

PACE. Pace is how fast or slow we talk. But it is more than that. A good speaker or conversationalist does not just talk fast or slow. He does both. His normal pace is somewhere in between - somewhere in the middle, but he picks up his pace or slows it down from time to time in order to gain increased attention from the listener.

"Speak clearly and have a pleasant voice" is what we've said in this section on voice. It's simple advice, but easier in concept than performance - easier to agree to in thought than to carry out in practice. But just about anyone can learn to use his voice effectively. Strong desire and lots of practice will get you there. Use a tape recorder and practice with friends who are eager to improve their own voice effectiveness.

Telephone Personality

We have just examined the importance of your voice in telephone communication. We turn now to look at the personality that you present when you are on the phone. There are four primary traits that are essential if you want to use the telephone effectively: (1) Alertness, (2) Friendliness, (3) Sincerity, (4) Confidence.

ALERTNESS. A fictional character was once described as always appearing "to be either just in the process of waking up, or right on the brink of falling asleep." When we say "alertness," this is not what we are looking for. You want the prospect or customer on the other end of the phone to see you as being wide-awake, lively, keen, sensitive, perceptive, interested, and responsive. In a word, you want the prospect to recognize immediately that you are a "live one" with all of your mental facilities "on go."

In the years before psychology became a science, there was a personality type called the "phlegmatic." It was described as being "not easily excited to action or display of emotion; having a calm or apathetic temperament." Today, we have our own adjectives for this kind of personality - dull, slow-witted, disinterested, lethargic. The personality marked by alertness is the polar opposite of the phlegmatic type. The alert person is lively, quick-witted, interested, and energetic - just the type of person a prospect or customer wants to talk with.

FRIENDLINESS. Most of us don't ever bother to define this trait, but we surely know it when we see it **or** when we **don't**! Friendliness is like a magnet; it attracts. Picture a friendly host and hostess at the front door of their home welcoming guests to a party. Their warm voices and smiling faces make the guests eager to enter and glad that they were invited.

A cluster of words describes several aspects of friendliness that the salesperson on the telephone wants to convey to the prospect or customer on the other end: pleasant, courteous, polite, attentive, caring, kind. If you don't think that these qualities are of the greatest importance, just consider how a prospect would feel if you dealt him their opposites. Imagine how a potential customer might respond to a salesperson who is **un**pleasant, **dis**courteous, **im**polite, **in**attentive, **un**caring, and **un**kind. Friendliness is always positive and proactive; never negative (unfriendly) or indifferent (unconcerned).

SINCERITY. Most prospects and customers are turned off instantly if they feel that they are "just being used" by a salesperson. Nobody likes to be exploited. Most successful salespersons learn early on that their own self-interest is best served when they make their customer's best interest their top priority. In other words, taking care of their customers takes care of themselves.

Most prospects can tell a phony, insincere salesperson "a mile off," but somehow insincerity over the telephone seems to get magnified. Maybe it's because all of the salesperson's props are missing - expensive clothes, slick handouts, fine-tuned body language, but on the phone there's just the naked message and it tends to show itself for what it is - a real diamond or a piece of worthless glass. Sincere means real, honest, genuine, natural. These aren't easy qualities to fake under any circumstances - in person or on the phone. So, if you have to "play act" all day every day in order to sell your product or service, either you're selling the wrong thing, or you don't belong in sales. The tip for you to take, if you intend to make a career out of sales is: "Get real or get out!"

CONFIDENCE. Every salesperson must deal with a wide variety of prospects and clients. Some of these persons will not be easy to handle, but it is extremely important for you to always present a positive mental attitude to the person with whom you are speaking. A brand new prospect may very quickly reveal that he will be a tough challenge to both your patience and your skill. Or a customer of longstanding with a track record for being a problem may alarm you when he calls. But you must always hide any anxiety that you have from the prospect or client. If you communicate, even unintentionally, any of your fear or doubt to the caller, he may see you as being vulnerable and raise the level of his attack or of his demand for concessions.

It's not an easy thing to sound genuinely enthusiastic about hearing from someone who in the past has always either scared you to death or made you mad as hell, but that's exactly what you must endeavor to do in negative situations like these. By being upbeat and talking positively, you may actually disarm an aggressive caller. In any case, you gain nothing, and more than likely lose ground, if you allow the customer to perceive that you are uncertain or fearful. Tell yourself: "I'm going to win this one," and go at it with a positive attitude. Your determination may just carry the day. If it doesn't, then the result comes as no surprise and you can take it in stride.

Answering the Phone and Getting Started

ANSWERING THE PHONE: HOW QUICKLY? There are opposing viewpoints about how quickly a salesperson should answer a phone. One school of thought insists that it should be answered on the first ring to demonstrate to callers how efficiently the company's office is run. A different point of view argues that to answer a phone on the first ring tells a prospect that the salesperson is like the Maytag repairman, just sitting around with nothing to do waiting for the phone to ring. Perhaps the best policy is a compromise between these two positions. Certainly you don't want a prospect to think that he's going to have to wait "all day" for somebody to answer the phone. On the other hand, you want to give the impression, which is no doubt also the truth, that you are a busy professional person with many people making demands on your time.

GREETING THE CALLER AND IDENTIFYING YOURSELF. As a salesperson at your office, you are answering a business phone, so naturally you need to say something more informative than "Hello." If you are answering a main or trunk line - that is, if the call is coming directly to you without having first gone through a receptionist or secretary - you need to identify your business, as well as yourself. You should also give the caller a prompt (cue) to tell you why he is calling - the nature of his business.

> *Example:* "Barlow's Trucking Service. This is Tim Stevens. How may I help you?"

If you are answering an extension line - a call that has been forwarded to you from a receptionist - then you need only give your name and the prompt which asks the caller what service he needs.

> *Example:* "This is Tim Stevens. How may I help you?"

GETTING THE CALLER'S NAME. Often it is a receptionist or secretary who will perform this task, but at smaller businesses salespersons frequently take customer calls directly. There are, of course, tactful and crude ways of asking a caller to identify himself. You want the prospect or customer to feel important, so you must ask for his name with a tone, and in a way, that does not intimidate him or send the wrong message. Hence, you would not just ask bluntly, "Who is this?" or "What's your name?" He must be made to sense that the request for his name is not a screen or a "test" aimed at keeping him from "getting through" and accomplishing his business in a timely manner. Instead, you want the prospect to feel that you are just trying to be efficient in forwarding his call to the proper person.

> *Example:* "I'll be glad to forward your call to Ms. Forsyth. May I tell her who is calling?

COVERING FOR ANOTHER SALESPERSON. Whether you are a receptionist, secretary, or salesperson, there will be times when you will have to talk with a prospect or customer who has called to speak with a salesperson who is not available or not in the office. How you handle this situation will either enhance or damage the image of the absent salesperson. There are all kinds of reasons why a salesperson may not be available to take a phone call - some of them personal, some of them professional.

You have no obligation to make a detailed accounting explaining the salesperson's unavailability to the caller, but it is important that you communicate to the prospect or client that the individual for whom he has called is busy taking care of business either in or out of the office and is simply not available "at this time." In addition, you should give the caller one or more options to choose from at the present moment. For example, the caller could speak with a sales assistant, another salesperson, or leave a message to have his call returned at a later time. Correct and incorrect ways of covering for an unavailable salesperson are given below.

Correct Example: "Ms. Covington is out of the office on an appointment right now. May I have her call you when she returns?"

Correct Example: "Ms. Covington is with another client right now. Would you like to speak with one of her sales assistants?"

Incorrect Example: "She hasn't called in yet this morning."

Incorrect Example: "She was here a while ago, but I don't know where she is now."

Interacting With the Caller

GENERALLY, DON'T INTERRUPT A CALLER. It is impolite to interrupt someone, but as a salesperson you have additional reasons for not interrupting a prospect or customer. Several negative things can happen when a prospect is interrupted:

- He may forget to describe some of his needs, thus depriving you of valuable cues for pitching particular features of your product or service.
- He may lose his train of thought and fail to state one or more objections which you could have overcome.
- He may think that you are not really listening to his argument or explanation.
- You may lose the advantage that comes from being perceived by the prospect as an objective and empathetic consultant.

INTERRUPT A CALLER WHEN YOU MUST. While it is generally true that you should not interrupt a prospect or client, there are rare occasions when interrupting an individual (usually a person who is already a customer) may be, from a strategic point of view, the correct thing to do. For example, the individual may be on a verbal rampage that has already gone on for two or three minutes without giving you an opportunity to respond to anything that he has said, his emotional state being ignited, rather than defused, by his outpouring of verbal abuse on you and your company. There is nothing for you to gain by continuing to be the passive recipient of his unrestrained outburst. In fact, you may even be able to turn the situation around if you make the right kind of interruption.

Example: "Excuse me..... Forgive me for interrupting,

Mr. Rustworth, but I really must respond to a couple of your concerns before you go any further. (He starts to continue his barrage of words.) Excuse me..... Excuse me, but you simply must allow me to answer two of the questions you have raised. (Pause.....) First of all, with regard to your concern about the price which you paid for ...."

As a salesperson, you must regain control of the conversation. If there are real problems that need to be solved, they must be focused upon and realistic solutions discussed. If you can convince the customer that you are willing to participate in a rational discussion of his complaints if he will simply agree to be civil, then you have set the stage for at least the possibility of some resolution to the situation.

In some instances it is necessary to interrupt a prospect or customer not because he is emotionally out of control but simply because he has drifted away from the central issues of the sales interview, and by so doing threatens to tie you up for the entire day or at least postpone indefinitely the possibility of your being able to close him. In such situations you must interrupt in order to reestablish the focus of the conversation.

> *Example:* "Excuse me, Mr. Frazzaling, excuse me, but I have an appointment in just a few minutes, and I know that you must have questions about my company's limited edition artworks that you haven't gotten answers to yet. For example, I'm sure that you would want to know that all of our signed "Artist's Proofs" lithographs are limited to just 250 prints per original artwork. I know that you must have some personal favorites among the several artists whose works we have reproduced. If you can just tell me....."

Here, the salesperson has the difficult task of getting the prospect back on track, and keeping him there. There is no conflict here as in the previous example, just a sales situation that has nearly aborted because of the prospect's case of the adult version of "Attention Deficit Syndrome."

DON'T TALK TOO MUCH. It's much easier to sell a prospect on your product or service if you know something about him. If you dominate the conversation, the prospect will no doubt discover a good deal about you, but your knowledge of him will not be increased very much. Many salespeople ramble on and on to the prospect, bruising the ears and trying his patience, and then try to close him without having learned anything about him or the kind of product or service he might be looking for. A skillful salesperson will draw out the prospect by asking leading questions, thus gaining valuable sales information for himself at the same time that he is being perceived as an intelligent and concerned professional by the prospect.

FOCUS AND CONFIRM. As a salesperson who sells on the telephone, you will not only make calls to prospects and customers; you will **receive** them. When you do, you should be careful to focus on what the prospect or customer is saying to you, not just on what you want to say to him. A customer who calls you certainly has a reason for calling. Find out what it is. Don't just rush blindly into a sales pitch, trying to resell him on what he's already bought. And don't jump to the conclusion that he's calling with a complaint or to tell you that he's changed his mind about making a purchase. Stay calm and positive, and listen to what he has to say. It may be **good** news. He may want to increase the size of his order or to buy additional products or services. After you've listened, confirm what he's said. Restate his message in your own words and ask him if you have it straight. You have nothing to lose and everything to gain by making a prospect or customer believe that you genuinely care about what he thinks and wants.

Most of the time, however, you will be **making** calls rather than receiving them. And of course you will have a sales presentation that you want to make; but if you don't encourage your prospects to interact with you and then pay attention to what they say - if you don't **focus** on their comments and questions and **confirm** your understanding of what they are saying - you won't make many sales.

LISTEN FOR A SUBLIMINAL MESSAGE. You can't always tell what a prospect is **really** thinking or feeling, especially on the telephone. You can't observe facial expressions or body language. But you **do** have more than just words to go by. Expression and inflection reveal boredom, indifference, curiosity, interest, or enthusiasm. An elevated (or rising) pitch usually indicates anger or excitement. A lowered pitch generally indicates a lack of enthusiasm or interest. Also, there is the speed or pace of a prospect's delivery. Increased pace often reveals either interest or anger, while a decreased pace usually indicates indecision, thoughtfulness, or low interest. By picking up on these subliminal clues, you can communicate more effectively with a prospect.

Technical Matters

BE READY TO DO BUSINESS. Selling on the telephone allows a salesperson to work at his own desk. This is a real plus. You can have everything you need to do business right at your fingertips - sales presentation script, features and benefits checklist, answers to objections, information fact sheets for the product or service you are selling, customer order or application forms, blank paper, note pads, etc.

Whether you are calling prospects or taking calls from customers, you are in a position to operate with maximum efficiency. Of course the experienced salesperson is **always** prepared, whether in the field or in his office, but there is **never** an excuse for any salesperson to be caught unprepared when he is working at his "home base."

PUTTING A PROSPECT OR CUSTOMER "ON HOLD." Many individuals are very sensitive to being put "on hold," and they have a right to be. Their time is as valuable (perhaps **more** valuable) as yours. Time is money, and you are wasting theirs when you have them "on hold." You need to train your assistants not to interrupt you when you are on the phone. They would not interrupt you if the prospect were sitting in your office, and they should not interrupt you just because he's "only on the phone." Still, for those times when you absolutely must put a person "on hold," you should have a phone equipped with a "hold" button so that you can actually cut off the line for a few moments. It is unprofessional to cover the phone mouthpiece with your hand, allowing the prospect or customer to hear garbled conversation at your end of the line.

"CALL WAITING." Call waiting" should not be used by salespersons. The person with whom you are already speaking will be aggravated by being put "on hold," and the incoming caller will not want to be put off by being told that you are presently busy with another person. It is a no-win situation for you. All too often a salesperson will take time to deal fully with a "call waiting," leaving the original caller "on hold" for perhaps 3-4 minutes. This is unthinkable!!! The original caller will be justifiably angered because you have allowed someone to jump in line ahead of him.

On the other hand, a secretary or receptionist should be able to use "call waiting" effectively and without offending any caller. People understand that business offices receive many calls and that a wait is sometimes necessary in order to reach the individual they have called. But once they have been "put through" to the salesperson they have been waiting to talk with, they **do not** want to be interrupted.

USING A "CONFIDENCER." If you work in an office where there is a lot of background noise or where managers sometimes coach salespersons who are talking with prospects, you need to have a "confidencer" on your phone. It is an inexpensive accessory that fits on the telephone mouthpiece and eliminates all background noise. It will save you from having to repeat yourself to prospects and customers who can't hear what you are saying.

HANG UP GENTLY. There are all kinds of reasons why you might slap down the receiver on your phone at the end of a call. Maybe you just made a big sale and can't wait to punch the air with your fist. Maybe you'd like to kill the cranky customer who just took 30 minutes of your time. Maybe you're just exhausted after a long day. Maybe you just weren't thinking. Whatever reason or excuse you might have for doing it, don't ever bang down the receiver when you hang up at the end of a call. If the prospect or customer at the other end of the line is still there, you are certain to startle, and probably offend, him.

Guidelines for Telephone Selling

The lists below are intentionally informal and incomplete, but they effectively suggest two very different profiles of the telephone salesperson. The contrasting profiles may seem to be oversimplified, but they can serve as dependable "channel markers" for even experienced salespersons who have lost their direction and need "navigational correction."

PROFILE OF A POSITIVE TELEPHONE SALESPERSON:

- Smile.
- Speak clearly and concisely.
- Be enthusiastic.
- Lower pitch of voice for friendly conversation.
- Talk in a positive way.
- Be prepared to answer objections.
- Talk directly into phone mouthpiece.
- Come to the point quickly.
- Explain features and benefits of product or service.
- Discuss.
- Thank prospect for listening to sales presentation.

PROFILE OF A NEGATIVE TELEPHONE SALESPERSON:

- Frown.
- Mumble.
- Be cynical.
- Speak in a monotone.
- Be negative.
- Be overbearing and scoff at questions.
- Talk with phone mouthpiece wedged under your chin.
- Ramble in a disorganized manner.
- Exaggerate the features and benefits of product or service.
- Argue.
- Slam phone receiver down if prospect says "No."

Consider the following questions as you review this chapter. Relate each question to your own routine for handling telephone sales calls.

25 TELEPHONE PERFORMANCE CHECKPOINTS:

1. How quickly do you answer your phone (trunk line or extension)?
2. How do you answer your phone?
3. How do you identify yourself and your company?
4. Is your opening statement appropriate for your company or business?
5. Do you interrupt a caller or fail to yield when a caller tries to interrupt you?
6. If a call is interrupted, do you leave the line and return to the line in a polite manner?
7. Are you attentive to and focused on what the caller is saying?
8. Do you express appreciation, concern, or regret when it is appropriate to do so?
9. Do you apologize if necessary?
10. Do you express in words or indicate by manner and tone a willingness to help?
11. Is your attitude friendly, helpful, and interested?
12. Does a caller receive your individual consideration or just routine treatment?
13. When information or explanations are needed, do you give them completely and precisely?
14. Do you use technical terms, slang words, or arbitrary statements?
15. Do you handle calls in a manner that builds confidence in the way your company is managed?
16. Does a caller who talks with you want to remain a customer of your company?
17. Do you make final arrangements of a sales transaction clear?
18. Do you respond appropriately to a caller's "Thank you" or other closing remarks?
19. Do you transfer calls thoughtfully and carefully?
20. Do you check to be sure that someone picks up a call that you have transferred?
21. Do you plan your calls ahead of time?
22. Do you listen for a dial tone before dialing, to be sure you don't interrupt another call?
23. Do you keep pens, pencils, and note pads close to your phone?
24. Do you hang the receiver up gently and securely?
25. Do you wait for the other party to hang up first?

Summary

As you gain experience in making and receiving telephone sales calls, you will soon discover that you are using the phone with much greater confidence. With every successful call, you'll find that confidence growing, and with it, the strong desire to be an even **more** effective telephone communicator. Remember to **analyze** all of your calls - the ones you make and the ones you receive. Ask yourself why one call was successful while another one was not. Identify the things you did right and the things you would change if you had the opportunity to handle a call again. Take notes on every call. Study the notes relating to successful calls and compare them with the notes on unsuccessful calls. See what conclusions you can draw. Of course the prospect or customer with whom you are dealing is always a factor in whether or not your call is successful. You can't win them all, but with the practice that comes from experience, and continuous study and analysis on your part, you are sure to become a winner in the field of telephone marketing.

3

DEVELOPING SOURCES

Introduction

How does a salesperson determine **who** to sell to? He sells to **prospects**. But **where** do they come from? How does he **find** them? Successful salespeople develop **prospect sources**. A prospect source is a base or pool from which a salesperson gathers potential buyers. This chapter explains how to develop prospect sources that will yield qualified prospects to buy the product or service that you are selling.

Prospect Source: Understanding the Concept

A "FISHING TALE" ANALOGY. Imagine for a moment that you are a sportsman who likes to fly-fish for largemouth bass. You have all the necessary gear for fishing, and you know **how** to fly-fish for your favorite game fish. You have the equipment and the know-how. You lack just one thing - the **place**. You are new to the area in which you now live, and so you must begin the process of discovering where, within practical reach of your new home, are the most productive lakes, ponds, rivers, and streams where you can catch largemouth bass. You need a **source** in order to engage in your favorite outdoor sport.

There are significant similarities between the situation of a salesperson and the situation of the fisherman just described. A salesperson may possess all of the "necessary gear" (a product or service to sell and an abundance of product information), may have the know-how required to accomplish his goal (years of sales experience), but, like the fisherman, needs a **source** in order to practice his art. The fisherman won't have a platter of fresh fish on his table if he doesn't find a place to catch them, and the salesperson won't make any sales if he doesn't have a source from which he can get prospects.

The Matchmaking Game: Your Product and a Prospect Source

TOYS, CANDY BARS, AND KIDS. It doesn't take rocket science to match most products with logical prospect sources. Take, for example, the companies who make toys, candy bars, soft drinks, and cereal. They know that their target audience is kids and that every Saturday morning huge numbers of kids watch cartoons on network television. So, it is not surprising that the makers of these products have for many years filled Saturday morning television with ads for their products.

The whole game is really pretty simple and very straightforward. You ask the question, "Who will buy my product or service?" You find out **where** those people are (prospect sources) and then start fishing (prospecting).

SOMETIMES IT'S TOUGH. The thing is, though, that it's **not always easy** to discover exactly where your prospect sources are. It depends on what you are selling - what your product or service is. Let's list a few things that people sell in order to explore this point a bit further.

- Life Insurance
- Personal Jewelry
- Commercial Real Estate
- Residential Pest Control Service
- Stocks and Mutual Funds
- Vitamins and Nutritional Food Supplements
- Fashion Dolls
- Dog Training Service
- Pet Supplies
- Home Security Systems
- Home Smoke Detectors
- Long Distance Telephone Service
- Agricultural Chemicals
- Hand-crafted Wood Benches and Picnic Tables
- Vinyl Siding Installation
- Miniature Bird and Animal Sculptures
- Swimming Pool Supplies
- Magazine Subscriptions

DIFFERENT PRODUCTS AND SERVICES: DIFFERENT PROSPECT SOURCES.
Obviously, the salespersons selling the various products and services listed above have very different tasks ahead of them when it comes to identifying their prospect sources. For example, the individual selling swimming pool supplies must come up with a list of people who own swimming pools. The target market here is finite (limited) and should yield a high percentage of sales once the list of names (prospect source) is obtained. But the salesperson will have to be creative in devising a method for coming up with the list that he needs. He can hardly do an aerial survey, and he certainly can't take the time required to drive from house to house looking in backyards.

There are additional products in the list above that have very limited prospect sources. Commercial real estate, fashion dolls, miniature bird and animal sculptures, and agricultural chemicals - all of these products have narrowly defined target audiences; but the salesperson who can successfully identify his prospect sources for one of these products can expect to achieve a good sales batting average.

On the other hand, some of the products and services listed above have almost infinite (unlimited) prospect sources. The prospect pool for salespeople who sell stocks and mutual funds, life insurance, personal jewelry, long distance telephone service, residential pest control service, vitamins and nutritional food supplements, magazine subscriptions, etc. is **huge**. The **challenge** to the salesperson selling a product or service which has an infinitely large prospect base is to discover **particular** prospect sources that will produce a relatively high percentage of buyers.

Ways to Make the Match... If Your Product Has a Narrow Prospect Base

UTILIZE SPECIALTY PUBLICATIONS. There are an amazing number of narrowly focused magazines and newsletters published in this country. Three of the products in the list above - personal jewelry, fashion dolls, and miniature bird and animal sculptures - probably fall into the category of collectibles that are promoted by one or more speciality publications. A visit with a librarian can get you started on the detective trail of the names and addresses of these publications. Most magazines and newsletters sell their subscriber lists for a nominal charge. Many hobby and collectible publications are glad to provide free subscriber and membership lists in order to promote their organizations.

GET MEMBERSHIP LISTS OF CLUBS AND ORGANIZATIONS. Local, regional, and national clubs and organizations represent countless special consumer interests. With reference to the products and services cited in the list above, the membership list of the regional kennel club would be of great value to individuals selling pet supplies and dog training services; the membership lists of local and regional antique and collectible groups would be helpful to persons selling fashion dolls, miniature bird and animal sculptures, and personal jewelry; membership lists of local and area swim clubs would no doubt be valuable to individuals selling swimming pool supplies; membership directories published by local and regional farm organizations would be of great importance to persons selling agricultural chemicals, etc. Chambers of Commerce and libraries can usually supply names and addresses of most local and area organizations.

OBTAIN INDIVIDUAL REFERRALS. Individual prospects and customers provide one of the best resources for building a prospect base. Even if their speciality interest has no publication or club, these individuals know the names of friends and associates who are fellow collectors and enthusiasts (of whatever). In most cases they will be glad to give you those names if they think that you have a product or service that will be of interest to their friends.

PLACE NEWSPAPER ADS. The classified advertising section of a newspaper can be used productively by individuals selling products or services that appeal to a narrow prospect base. For example if you are selling fashion dolls, personal jewelry, or miniature bird and animal sculptures, an ad placed in the "Antiques & Collectibles" section of the classified ads may net you valuable responses. Similarly, if you are selling dog training services or pet supplies, an ad under the "Pets & Supplies" banner may serve you well.

GO AFTER NEW ENTHUSIASTS. The four suggestions above are rooted in the idea that you are simply trying to discover the narrow prospect source (base) that already exists for the product or service that you are selling. But you should not fail to consider the possibility that there are large prospect sources "out there" that are just waiting to be attracted to your product or service. For example, bankers, dentists, greenhouse owners, and firemen may all represent potentially fruitful markets for the sale of dog training services. It may be that very few individuals from these four groups belong to the local kennel club, but that doesn't exclude them from being potential consumers of dog training services.

We can envision another example of this type by focusing on fashion dolls and miniature bird and animal sculptures. It may be that there are virtually no collectors of either of these products among the owners and customers of local dress shops and beauty salons, but that doesn't equate to the fact that there is no sales potential for these items among those two groups. The point is that salespersons who deal in products or services that have very narrow existing prospect bases, can always make the decision to target **new** audiences with the idea of gaining "converts" and new enthusiasts for the product or service they are selling.

Ways to Make the Match ...... If Your Product Has a Broad Prospect Base

If you sell a product or service that has a very broad, virtually unlimited, prospect base, you can be sure of one thing - there are many other salespeople competing with you, selling the same product or service. Therefore, your challenge is not to discover a large number of prospect groups (They've already been discovered), but rather, to find prospect audiences that have not already been worked to death by other salespersons. Listed below are several suggestions worth trying.

CULTIVATE FRESH SOURCES. A young stock broker in Florida felt the need to develop a new prospect source. Driving to appointments in the outlying areas adjacent to the city in which his office was located, he observed that there were many dairy farms. They appeared to be large, prosperous operations. Most likely the owners of these farms had money to invest. He doubted that dairy farmers, as a group, had been targeted as a prospect source by local investment brokers.

He decided to research the situation and discovered that the typical dairy farmer in his area had a high net worth but, due to current high feed costs and low wholesale milk prices, was struggling with cash-flow problems. As a stock broker, he knew that he had what the dairy farmer needed - a proven way to get a higher return on his investments so that he would have more available cash to get through his short-term business squeeze. He decided to target the dairy farmers as a prospect source. But before he started talking with any of them, he gathered valuable information about the industry from local commercial and government offices. The questions below are a sampling of the ones he asked.

  - What is the size of the average dairy farm?
  - How many cows are on the average farm?
  - What is considered to be a small dairy farm? A large one?
  - Do most of the farms belong to co-ops?
  - What are the current wholesale milk prices?
  - What are current wholesale feed prices?
  - What are the projected trends for wholesale milk and feed prices?
  - Do local dairy farmers have out-of-state competition?
  - Does the dairy industry have an oversupply problem? A shortage problem?
  - What are the three biggest concerns facing local dairy farmers?

By getting the answers to these and other questions the investment broker was able to "talk the talk" of the dairy farmers. He opened up a virtually untapped local prospect source, getting many referrals from inside the group.

DO CREATIVE AND UNUSUAL ADVERTISING. There are ways to spend your advertising dollars that enable you to reach prospect audiences that will actually **appreciate** your ads. Listed below are advertising ideas that target friendly, receptive prospect groups.

  - Place billboard ads at city recreation sports fields, Little League parks, etc.

  - Sponsor local sports teams and put your business name on the uniforms.

  - Buy display ads in the "Program" for the performances sponsored by local music, dance, and theater organizations.

  - Purchase ad space in publications sponsored by local museums, historical societies, etc.

- Put an ad for your product or service on place mats and provide them free of charge to local restaurants

- Pay for the printing of "Fire Safety" fliers for a Volunteer Fire Department and put your advertisement for home smoke detectors on the back.

There is no end to the number of creative ways you can spend your advertising dollars. The key to success in this area, of course, is to target prospect groups who (1) will appreciate your advertising, (2) have money to spend on your product or service, and (3) are not already flooded with advertisers.

PLACE LEAFLETS AND BROCHURES AT STRATEGIC PLACES. Direct mail advertising campaigns net a very low percentage of respondents or prospects. There is nothing surprising about this since the direct mail strategy is a very broad-brush approach to advertising. But leaflets or brochures promoting your product or service placed strategically at sites where favorably disposed individuals will see them (and pick them up) can bring you many positive inquiries from self-qualified prospects. Listed below are several examples of how to match your product or service to a site (place of business).

- Hand-crafted Wood Benches and Picnic Tables
    Place advertising fliers at Landscape & Nursery Businesses.

- Dog Training Service
    Place advertising fliers at Veterinary Offices and Hospitals.

- Fashion Dolls / Miniature Bird and Animal Sculptures
    Place advertising fliers in Jewelry Stores.

- Pest Control Service
    Place advertising fliers at Home Improvement / Hardware Stores.

- Vitamins and Nutritional Food Supplements
    Place advertising fliers in Offices of Physicians / Physical Therapists.

The key to this advertising strategy, of course, is finding a **close** match-up between your product or service and the business or professional outlet where you place your advertising materials. In some cases you won't be able to place your fliers at the **perfect** site because that particular business sells the **same** product or service. Naturally, such a business will not be willing to supply you with advertising space for your competing product or service. For example, a Home Improvement Store sells wood picnic tables and benches; understandably, they will not want to display your fliers for the same product. But, as suggested above, a Landscape Nursery Business which does **not** sell picnic tables and benches will probably be glad to display your advertising leaflets.

TARGET SPECIAL-NEED PROSPECT GROUPS. Targeting special-need prospect audiences is not a new idea, but precisely because it has been around such a long time (long enough to have been discounted by many salespeople), there may be good reason to give it fresh consideration. Life insurance agents once kept a daily record of births, deaths, and weddings announced in local newspapers. They saw sales opportunities in these prospect sources. Parents of a newborn were seen as prime prospects for purchasing an annuity to provide for the child's college expenses. Newlyweds were encouraged to buy insurance protection to guarantee each other's long-term financial security. Widowed spouses were counseled in the investment of money newly acquired as the result of their loved one's death.

Births, deaths, and weddings, however, are not the only special events that define prospect groups. There are other significant life-cycle events that salespeople should take note of. For example:

- High School Graduation
- College or University Graduation
- Divorce
- Career Advancement (Job Promotion)
- Purchase or Construction of a New Home
- Opening or Selling of a Business
- Selling Property or a Home
- Retirement
- Making a Large Charitable Donation
- Birth of Grand-children
- Announcement of Major Travel Plans

These are only some of the "marker" events which individuals experience. Each salesperson must decide for himself, based upon the product or service that he sells, which, if any, of these events might define an individual as a prospect.

USE CLASSIFIED ADS IN NEWSPAPERS. This doesn't sound like a brand new idea! But many people in sales today never consider using small classified ads. They think that only large block or display ads get the attention of prospects. But the truth is that many people read "the classifieds" closely when they are looking for a particular product or service. Most newspapers today provide very specific categorical headings to organize the ads, making them user-friendly for potential buyers. For example, the following products and services selected from the list at the beginning of this chapter can all be advertised under narrowly descriptive headings in almost any contemporary city newspaper:

- Vinyl Siding Installation
- Pest Control Service
- Home Security Systems
- Home Smoke Detectors
- Hand-crafted Wood Benches and Picnic Tables

A well written classified ad can bring a prospect audience to you for very **little cost** and with the investment of almost **no time** on your part - two very important factors for any salesperson operating on a limited budget and lacking enough time to adequately cover his daily work load.

GET REFERRALS FROM PROSPECTS AND CUSTOMERS. Regardless of what you sell, and whether you get prospects from a narrow or broad prospect base, you should always ask prospects and customers for referrals. You can be sure that they will not give you the names of persons who have no interest in what you are selling; they don't want to catch flack from their friends. So, when you get referrals, you usually get **qualified** prospects.

USE YOUR TELEPHONE BOOK. A skillful carpenter can take a hammer and saw and the necessary building materials and build a house, but that doesn't mean that just **anybody** can do the same thing. Many salespersons get only minimal benefits from their phone book(s), but an intelligent and focused sales professional can get an amazing amount of mileage from a city phone book.

Many telephone directories, in addition to the white and yellow pages, now have blue (or green, etc.) pages with listings for local, state and national government offices and agencies. These pages can be very helpful to salespeople since many government offices publish informational bulletins and directories of various kinds that can serve as valuable resources for salespersons trying to research particular industries and develop prospect sources.

Today's Yellow Pages in many city phone books have an automated, free-access, interactive, expanded information service that can be dialed by punching in information-request codes for products and services advertised in the Yellow Pages. Many phone books also have special color-coded pages which list and explain "Community Services." The white pages, of course, appear in today's phone books as they always have - an undifferentiated mass of unqualified, potential prospects capable of spending billions of dollars annually for the purchase of products and services. Some salespeople scorn the phone book as a sales tool that belongs to the past, but many businesses have been built on it; and more individuals use the telephone for selling today than ever before.

USE YOUR LIBRARY. Many salespersons shy away from going to a library; and if they ever **do** go, it is only to read business magazines and newspapers. They are unaware that most libraries have extensive holdings of business reference books and directories. Some of these cover businesses and individuals in a single state; others are national in scope. A sampling of the diverse coverage afforded by various of these business directories is listed below:

- Building Contractors
- College & University Alumni
- Industries
- Chambers of Commerce
- Government Agencies
- College & University Faculty
- Church Members
- Furniture Manufacturers
- Metalworking Companies
- Bar Associations
- Physicians
- Retail Shopping Malls
- Veterinarians
- Law Enforcement Agencies
- Nursing Homes
- Real Estate Agents
- State Parks
- Ski Resorts
- Automobile Dealers
- Newspapers
- Environmental Organizations
- Civic Clubs

- Small Businesses
- Accounting Firms
- Country Clubs
- Churches
- Industrial Parks
- Retail Businesses
- Wholesale Businesses
- Camping and RV Parks
- Mobile Home Dealers
- Employment Agencies
- Hospitals
- Antique Dealers
- Funeral Directors
- Pilots
- Builders Associations
- Travel Agents
- National Parks
- Professional Engineers
- Life Insurance Companies
- Architects
- Dentists
- Motel Owners

Remember, this is only a sampling of what can be found in the business directories in your public library. If you live in a small town or city, you may have to go to a larger city to find a library that has the directories that will be most helpful to you. Plan to spend time (and money!) at the copying machine because business directories cannot be checked out; they are considered reference books and are kept in the library at all times. Once you have initiated yourself into the fine art of using your library's business resources, you will wonder how you ever got along without them.

GET CHAMBER OF COMMERCE GUIDES. Few salespersons overlook the directories that are available from local Chambers of Commerce. However, many fail to use them effectively after they obtain them. Too, depending on what product or service you sell, you may be helped by these tools whereas someone else was not. In any case, almost every local Chamber of Commerce publishes a "Directory" and a "Buyer's Guide." They list business names and types, owner and manager's names, and the business address and phone number.

CONSIDER MAGAZINE SUBSCRIBER LISTS. Many magazines, trade journals, and newsletters sell subscriber lists. If there is a publication (or several) that focuses directly on what you sell, you might profit from buying its subscriber list. Most magazines charge from 10-20 cents per name with a minimum purchase of 5,000 - 10,000 names, but cost per name and size of minimum order accepted varies greatly from magazine to magazine. If you do face-to-face selling, rather than telemarketing, you should inquire to see if you can buy names from particular cities or from a single state.

CONSIDER "GUIDES TO DIRECTORIES." There are literally "Directories to Directories." They are expensive (around $200 for some) and very comprehensive (as in **big**!) and may go beyond anything that is practical for your particular business. But, depending on what you sell and the scope of your sales enterprise, you might want to consider buying one. Two of these "super" directories are noted below:

- "Directories in Print," published by Gale Research, contains the names of about 10,000 lists and sources.
- "The Guide to American Directories," published by Bernard Klein, has brief descriptions of each directory included. The directories cover a variety of markets - industrial, commercial, occupational, and private.

Summary

There are so many possibilities when it comes to identifying and developing sources that will yield real prospects for any salesperson that it is difficult to point to any single idea or technique that might be described as the *surefire thing to do* for anyone seeking to discover new and worthwhile prospect sources. But there are two things - two guidelines - that every salesperson should always keep in mind when it comes to the business of looking for new sources: (1) Be creative and imaginative, and (2) Be persistent.

As we have seen in this chapter, the salesperson who comes up with a *new* or *uncultivated* source gains a real advantage over his competitors. The individual who works really hard prospecting a source that has *already* been prospected by twenty of his competitors cannot expect much success in identifying new prospects. But the individual who puts his finger on a source that none of his competitors have thought of will gain the great advantage that comes to the salesperson who is "breaking new ground" - talking to *new* people who have not already been "sorted through" by dozens of salespersons who got there first.

The second thing that every successful salesperson does with regard to looking for new prospect sources is that he does it *all the time*. Reading the daily newspaper, watching television, driving to an appointment, shopping at the mall, taking the kids to a soccer game - the superior individual is always looking for new, untouched prospect sources. Creativity and imagination *count* here. All of his competitors do the same things, see the same things, go the same places, but they wear the blinders of traditional thinking about where (and how) prospect sources are discovered, so, to paraphrase the well-known saying from ancient wisdom, "They have eyes to see, but see not; ears to hear, but hear not." The individual who comes up with new, uncultivated sources will be the salesperson who gets ahead and *stays* ahead because creativity and imagination *do* count!

4

PROSPECTING AND QUALIFYING

In the previous chapter we spent a good deal of time exploring various ways to develop prospect sources - particular audiences or populations that a salesperson can sort through for the purpose of identifying qualified prospects. This present chapter focuses on the process or procedure by which a salesperson refines or distills a large **prospect source** down to a smaller **qualified prospect list.**

A SWEET ANALOGY. The whole business of prospecting and qualifying is a lot like the matter of looking for your favorite chocolates in a two-pound sampler box. You like only the ones that have fruit centers, or cream centers, or nuts, or whatever; but you can't tell by just looking at them in the box; they all look so much alike. So you have to test each one, a nibble here, a small bite there; more often disappointed than rewarded. But, oh the joy of finding the ones you like - the ones with the chewy tart orange centers (or whatever)! It's **just** that way with an undifferentiated (unsampled, untested, unprobed) prospect source or group; you have to **check it out** in order to know which individuals in that group are "live ones" with the need for and the ability to buy your product or service.

Prospecting and qualifying is what you, as a salesperson, have to do (usually on the phone) in order to come up with a list of persons who are in actual fact (not just in your wishful thinking) potential customers - potential buyers for your product or service. Prospecting and qualifying is your calling and talking with individuals from a source group (that you have targeted) for the purpose of discovering which of them are **real prospects** and which are not.

THE IMPORTANCE OF PROSPECTING. Remember, whether you are a new salesperson or an experienced veteran, there is always attrition in your business - a certain number of customers (and their accounts) who disappear every year. Sometimes you will know what happened to them and why; sometimes you won't. But the bottom line is that you will have to replace them. In fact, a good rule of thumb is that in order to keep your volume of business growing, you should try to replace every old account that you lose with two new ones.

SET YOUR ATTITUDE. The verb "set" may seem like the wrong word to use with reference to your attitude, but probably it is not. We set the timer on a microwave oven; we set the dials on dishwashers and clothes dryers. We set timers and dials on household appliances to make them do **want** we want them to do, to make them **work** for us. And that is just what we have to do with our attitude before we start making prospecting phone calls; we have to **set** it so that it will work **for** us, not **against** us. We have discussed already in the "Communication" and "Telephone Performance" chapters (1 & 2) the importance of the personality (attitude) that you communicate to prospects. But we should reiterate here that a positive mental outlook is a major plus for the individual who is just sitting down to do several hours of telephone prospecting and qualifying.

EXPECT SUCCESS. If you **expect** success, you are more likely to **get** it. The positive and optimistic tone that you communicate to the person you are calling has the power to generate his interest. When you sit down to call 75 prospects, you should not think of the group as being made up of 60 individuals who will say "No" and 15 who will say "Yes." That sort of outlook on your part defines your role as passive or static, rather than active and dynamic. Only a few of the persons in the group will make "pre-determined" responses. The majority will be **affected** by you - your personality, your communication skills, and the information you deliver.

DON'T BE UPSET BY A "NO." You are certain to get negative responses from **some** of the prospects you call. (If they all said "Yes," you would be a billionaire overnight!) Remember **why** you are making all of these phone calls; you are making them in order to sort out the individuals who are **real** prospects from those who are not. Each time you get a "No," you are simply eliminating one more individual that you will waste no further time on, giving you that much more time to focus your attention on live prospects rather than deadwood.

DRESS FOR SUCCESS. How you look is not important to a prospect on the other end of the phone line, but it may very well be important to **you**. If you are dressed like a successful professional, you probably will **feel** like one. And, of course, how you feel **will** be communicated to the prospect on the phone. Personal appearance - clothes and grooming - is discussed at length in "Chapter 5" ("The Appointment").

KNOW YOUR PRODUCT. Nothing can give you more confidence than knowing your product or service inside and out. Knowing your product enables you to explain to a prospect **why** he should be interested in it. You should be an expert on the product you are selling. The questions below suggest the kind of information you should know. If you are selling a service, you should have the answers to similar questions.

- What does the product do?
- How much does it cost?
- How does it work?
- How much money can it make (or save) for the end-user?
- What are its main features or capabilities?
- Are there important things (functions) it can't do (perform)?
- Does it have features that competing products lack?
- What are the three biggest positives about your product?
- What are the three biggest negatives?
- To whom are you marketing your product?
- What is the profile of your typical customer or prospect?
- What kinds of problems will your product solve for a customer?
- How can it solve them?
- Why should a prospect buy your product?
- Will there be a maintenance cost? How much?
- What is the product's life expectancy?

Having the answers to these kinds of questions will allow you to engage an interested prospect in a substantive dialog about your product. The most unforgivable sin a salesperson can commit is not being able to respond intelligently to an interested prospect's question. There's no point in making prospecting phone calls if, quite literally, "you don't know what you're taking about."

PREPARE A WRITTEN SCRIPT. You need to keep in mind that not every prospect is just sitting by his phone anxiously waiting for you to call. That being the case, you need to consider the format and content of your prospecting/qualifying presentation. You must envision an individual who is **not** eager to receive your call - an individual who tends to be skeptical, perhaps even cynical, about "telephone salespeople." What will it take to engage this person in friendly and lively conversation? What will it take to move this individual along toward a positive and inquiring attitude about the product or service you are selling? These are considerations that you must take into account as you prepare a script for your prospecting presentation.

You have to believe that there are poor, fair, good, better, and best quality scripts that can be written for your prospecting/qualifying phone presentation. It's your responsibility (and challenge!) to develop a "best" quality script. You'll be able to fine-tune your script as you use it, but **don't** start making prospecting phone calls without having spent serious time developing the best presentation possible.

Many salespersons think that there's something phony or unprofessional about using a script. But the bottom line is that by developing a carefully thought-out presentation, you're simply applying your intelligence to a difficult task rather than just "playing it by ear," or, to put it more picturesquely (and accurately!), "flying by the seat of your pants." Remember that television's national network news "anchors" are paid millions of dollars a year to "sound spontaneous" while reading a script.

Have all your business "tools" close at hand

It's important to have everything that you might need during a prospecting phone call conveniently located so that you will not have to interrupt the flow of your dialog with a prospect in order to "find" something. You should have pens, pencils, blank paper, business forms, prospect information cards (or forms), etc. within easy reach on your desk top. Imagine how you would be put off by a workman who came to your home to do a project and then left in just a few minutes because he had forgotten some of his tools. When you call a prospect, you lay claim to a piece of his time; if you waste it by not having all of your business "tools" at your fingertips, you probably will lose the prospect.

Planning and Managing Your Prospecting and Qualifying

DEVELOP AN OVERALL PLAN OR STRATEGY FOR PROSPECTING. Although some salespersons will tell you that they are "always prospecting," that really doesn't accurately describe how most successful individuals go about the task. The fact is that there will be cycles or periods of time when you will need to develop (enlarge) your pool of prospects. At such a point in time you may develop 200 new prospects, but then you will need time to "work" those prospects. Obviously, there is no value in developing a pool of 900 new prospects if you don't have time to convert them from prospects to customers. So, you need to have an overall plan or strategy for developing new prospects when that particular task is your top priority.

SELECT PROSPECT SOURCES. In the previous chapter (#3) we discussed how to develop prospect sources. Remember that a source is a target group, a population or audience from which you hope to gather prospects. So now you need to select the sources you want to prospect. You may decide that you will focus on dentists, opticians, and accountants. Once you have picked your source groups, you must obtain or compile a list of names and phone numbers for each group.

There is a particular benefit that you derive from prospecting homogeneous sources - groups consisting of individuals that share a common occupation or profession. If you are prospecting dentists "all at once" (rather than a few at a time over a period of several months), you will quickly discover how their needs as a professional group relate to the product or service that you are selling. You will also pick up on (and learn to use) certain words and phrases that distinguish the group's professional jargon. Talking with only 2-3 dentists a month would not afford you with this advantage that comes from intense daily contact with professional persons belonging to a single group.

PRIORITIZE SOURCES. You must decide which of your source groups you will prospect first, second, third, etc. Generally, salespersons assign top priority to the source that they feel will yield the best percentage of prospects. So, if you feel that your product or service will have more appeal to accountants than to dentists and opticians, then prospect the accountants first. The governing concept at work here is that you want to secure the **maximum** number of new prospects by making the **minimum** number of phone calls.

SET GOALS. When you are beginning a period of intense prospecting, you will need to decide on the number of new prospects that you want to develop and the time frame in which you want to secure them. You might, for example, decide that you want to gain 200 viable prospects in a 3-week period. That would equate to 13-14 new prospects per day for the 15 regular work days of the projected 3-week period. If these numbers seem unobtainable, then you would want to revise your goals, either lowering the number of prospects to be discovered, or extending the time frame for securing them.

SCHEDULE FULL DAYS OF PROSPECTING. If prospecting and qualifying is your top work priority for a period of time, schedule **whole** days for being on the phone. Prospecting is always a percentage operation. If you dedicate only a few hours a day to it, you may go several days without benefitting psychologically from the "positive probability rhythm" that tends to show up more readily when you prospect 8-10 hours a day.

DON'T WASTE TIME SORTING UNDIFFERENTIATED SOURCES. If you're prospecting accountants and you don't know anything about any of them, don't waste time trying to prioritize names in order to establish a calling sequence. **Just start calling!** If your list is alphabetized, start with the "A's." If it's not, start with the first name on the first page. Any "educated guesses" you might make as to which individuals are "most likely" and which ones "least likely" are really just that - **guesses**. Forget the "educated" and get busy!

BE STRATEGIC IN TIMING CERTAIN CALLS. As a general rule you will prospect businesses during the day and personal residences at night. But there is more to it than that. For example, you are not likely to score points with a restaurant owner or manager if you call during lunch or dinner hours. Similarly, a dentist will probably not have time to talk with you between 8:00 and 3:00. But there is no law against calling a business or professional person at home after 6:00 in the evening. The whole thing is that you must be creative in timing your calls to certain individuals.

Many successful professional persons are in their offices 2-3 hours before their business opens its doors to the public. The salesperson who calls a merchant, a real estate broker, a building contractor, or a health professional at 6:30 or 7:00 in the morning will find that he is not screened out by a receptionist or secretary. He may **also** discover that the prospect is amazed (and impressed!) by his work ethic. There are many stories of business owners who have responded to a salesperson's early-morning call by saying, "Look, I don't need what you're selling, but if you ever want a job, come talk to me. I like your hustle!"

KEEP RECORDS OF YOUR PROSPECTING. You cannot call hundreds of individuals on source lists and hope to keep your information about them "straight" if you don't have a good record keeping system.

USE PROSPECT CARDS. Prospect cards can be purchased from many business and office supply stores, or you can make your own. Many salespersons like the 4 X 6 size since they are large enough to hold a lot of information, yet small enough to keep in a portable, desktop size file box. The card should have headings and spaces that provide for the prospect's name, phone number, address, business or professional connection, and product or service needs. You can always write additional personal information on the back of the card.

DEVELOP A MEANINGFUL FILING SYSTEM. Experienced salespersons know that prospect cards are virtually worthless unless they are filed in a meaningful way. One effective method is to sort them according to the "type of product or service" the prospect is interested in. If you sell several different products or services, you need to be able to quickly access information that will tell you which prospects are interested in Product "A" or Service "B," etc. But then you may have 65 prospects who have indicated an interest in Product "A." Are they all equally interested? Certainly not. So, you need to tab the cards in each section of your product and service files according to the prospect's "level of interest." For example, you could use red tabs for hot prospects, yellow for lukewarm, and green (as in cemetery grass) for individuals who have expressed a passive kind of interest.

DON'T FILE INFORMATION ON UNQUALIFIED PROSPECTS. If an individual (1) expresses an interest in a product or service that you sell, (2) has the authority to make the buy-decision, and (3) has the financial ability to make the purchase, then he is a **qualified** prospect. Write him up and file his prospect card appropriately as indicated above. If an individual does not meet the three criteria just cited, then he is **not** a qualified prospect and should not be written up. You don't want a file full of names of individuals who will never buy your product or service. Worse, you don't want to waste time in the future by making second and third phone calls to them!

Don't keep deadwood in your files. If a prospect tells you that he can do business with you within 60 days, write him up, put a "suspense" (temporary) tab on the card, and file it. Follow up with second and third phone calls. If you discover that he will not make a purchase within 60 days, remove his card from your file. On the other hand, if a prospect tells you that he will **not** be able to buy your product or service within 60 days, simply drop his name from your source list. Don't fill out a prospect card for him.

Use a computerized data management package. If you have a computer, you may want to use a store-bought data management package to keep records of your prospecting and other sales activities. Most available software packages will accommodate the input of the kind of data that we have discussed above and can sort and print it for you according to your command.

Guidelines for Managing the Prospecting Phone Call

Develop a two-way dialog with the prospect to engage his interest and to obtain   information about his product or service needs.

Use clear words and sentences that sound natural and are easy to understand.

Encourage interruptions (questions and comments) by the prospect, but move smoothly back to your script after responding to the prospect.

Describe the benefits of your product or service in concrete, specific terms.

Avoid exaggerating the benefits of your product or using vague statements and half-truths to describe it.

Maintain control of the conversation by smooth and subtle management of the prospect's focus, but do not allow him to feel that he is being "pushed" or given a "hard sell."

Structure attention-grabbing statements into your presentation; use concise factual statements that you can expand on if the prospect responds.

Don't overwhelm the prospect by giving him too much information too soon.

Respond to particular interests or needs of the prospect during the course of the   conversation by describing relevant features and benefits of your product or service.

Be sure to present all major benefits of your product. You want to give the prospect every opportunity to respond positively so that you can qualify him as an individual that you will cultivate further.

The 5-Part Script for the Prospecting Phone Call

Earlier in this chapter we mentioned the importance of writing out the prospecting presentation. It should have five parts as indicated below.

Part 1.   Greet the prospect.
        Say "Hello," "Good morning," "Good afternoon," etc.

Call him by name.
        Use his whole name, or last name only with the prefix of Mr. or Ms. Some salespersons use first names, but many prospects will be put off by being addressed so informally (presumptively) by a total stranger who wants to sell them something.

Identify yourself.
        Give your first and last names. ("Brenda Walker," "Tom Smith," etc.)
Identify your business and its location.
        If your business is local, and if the prospect indicates an interest, tell him exactly where your office is. You want him to feel familiar with your operation.

Say that you know he's busy.
        (Don't ask if you've interrupted his work or a project or whatever; that gives him the opportunity to say, "Yes" and hang up.)   He will probably respond to the above statement by saying, "Yes, I really am, and I don't have time to ....."   Politely but quickly cut him off by saying something like, "I was sure you would be working on a tight schedule. I am, too, so I'll get right to the point."

Part 2.   Declare that you are only calling to introduce yourself and your company, not to sell him a particular product or service.

Ask if he is familiar with your company and its products or services. Unless you represent a "Fortune 500" company or a business with local headquarters (or factory), he probably will answer "No." That's just what you want to hear; it opens the door to the next stage of your presentation.

PART 3. Describe your company and the product or service that you sell. If the prospect has allowed you to go this far, you can be sure that you have an audience for at least a few minutes. It's up to you to concisely showcase your company and its product or service in a way that will engage the prospect and secure his interest.

PART 4. Describe a particular aspect of your company's operation (or one of its products or services) that is unusual and/or outstanding. By this point in the phone conversation you should have picked up on one (or more) interests or needs of the prospect. Try to match your company's (or product or service's) strength to the need which the prospect has revealed.

Make a strong summary statement about your company's overall strength, performance, dependability, etc. You want to leave the prospect on a high note regarding the stature and quality of your company.

PART 5. Remind the prospect that you called only to introduce yourself and your company and to discover if he has any particular needs.

If the prospect volunteers a need, qualify him further so that you can make a specific recommendation, and close him. On the other hand, if he does not indicate any particular need, thank him for his time, tell him you will be in touch, and hang up.

A Sample Prospecting Phone Call

"Hello! Frank Thomas? This is Angela Clark with Xanthia Printing Company here in Rochester. How are you?"

(Pause)

"I hope I didn't catch you at a bad time - in a conference or a meeting. I know you must have a busy schedule just as I do, but I wanted to call you to introduce myself and my company which has just opened an operation here. Have you seen our new plant on the west side of the Cloverdale Mall?"

(Pause)

"Yes, well, I'm not surprised that you're not familiar with Xanthia. Like I said, we're new to Rochester. But I think it won't be long before we become a household word around here, at least with businesses like yours. We're a "new generation" printing company, computer driven and ......"

(Pause)

"No, no, I'm glad you asked. I'll be pleased to explain. You see our entire printing operation is based on computer input. All work orders are developed on a computer system which interfaces with our state of the art electronic printing equipment. Our high-tech facility enables us to get projects out about three times faster than most traditional printing plants. It also ..... I'm sorry, go right ahead."

(Pause)

"Not at all. That's a logical question, but the truth is that with our computer driven operation we really don't have to give any consideration to the **size** of a job. The man-hours required for any particular project, regardless of its size or volume, are minimized by our high-tech system; so we can afford to print small orders at **almost** the same per-unit rate that we charge for much larger orders. And we **never** reject an order because of its size."

(Pause)

"Well, yes, there is **more** to our story. There are a couple of things that our system allows us to do for customers that are kind of special. Once we have input your order into our system, we can provide you almost immediately with a draft copy to examine and modify. Then, based on your recommendations, we can "tweak" the project wherever necessary so that it complies precisely with your vision of how it should look."

"Another special thing that we can do for our customers is to accept their printing orders directly on our computer system. For example, we can provide you with the specs for the procedure that allows you to send a project to us via your computer modem. This capability of our system saves you time and money because we can get started on your project without ever dealing with hard copy."

(Pause)

"Well, of course! I'd be happy to come to your office and give you more details about the various ways we might be able to save you time and money on your printing projects. How about next Tuesday. Will that work for you?"

Techniques for Enhancing the Prospecting Phone Call

There are many things that you can do to improve your batting average when you prospect on the phone. Some of the most important are discussed below.

BE WARM AND PERSONAL. Even though you use a script for your prospecting phone calls, you can avoid sounding cold and machine-like. You must **not** sound like you are reading or reciting from memory; nothing could be more impersonal. If you can project a warm, conversational tone to your prospects, you will probably double the percentage of positive responses that you get. Another thing: don't stumble over a prospect's name. Pronounce it out loud a couple of times before you dial the call. If it's an unusually difficult name, discuss it with an associate it before you make the call. It's hard to sound caring and personal if you can't pronounce a prospect's name correctly.

AVOID DISTRACTIONS. Making effective prospecting phone calls is very difficult work and requires intense concentration. Your effectiveness will be greatly diminished if you allow yourself to be distracted by anything that takes away from a 100% focus on the prospect. If you do not have a private and quiet office environment from which you can make your calls, then you will have to learn to **mentally isolate** yourself from everything around you - other people, office noises, etc. Also, any personal or business concerns that may be competing for your attention must be put on "hold" while you are engaged in prospecting. Think of yourself as a baseball player standing at the plate with your total attention riveted upon the pitcher who is about to deliver the ball. You cannot afford to divert even a small amount of your attention in any other direction.

DON'T DEVIATE FROM YOUR SCRIPT. After making several back-to-back calls, you may begin to feel that your script is old and repetitive. Remind yourself that it is brand new to each prospect you call. They are hearing it for the first time. You worked hard to develop your script, and it's worth using **just as it is**. Any departures that you make from it should occur only when you have to respond directly to questions or comments from the prospect. You may become harried and frustrated after several hours on the phone, but just continue to trust the careful planning that you put into the script under much less stressful circumstances.

DON'T LET CALLS END QUICKLY. If you find that your calls are ending abruptly or before you have gotten very far into your scripted presentation, take a short break and regroup. You know before you start a day of telephone prospecting that many individuals will not be interested in your product or service and probably will not allow you to get through your full script. But if you start getting a run of quick cut-offs or hang-ups, then you need to take a break and reenergize yourself. Don't be alarmed; it's only natural that after many back-to-back calls, your enthusiasm level will fall off a bit. Rest your brain and voice for a few minutes, walk down the hall and back a couple of times - whatever - and then get back on the phone with new energy!

END EVERY CALL ON A POSITIVE NOTE. One thing that you can be absolutely sure of is that every call you make will uncover a prospect who is either interested in or **not** interested in the product or service that you are selling. You have nothing to gain by "burning bridges" with prospects who respond negatively to your call. Thank them for their time and warmly wish them a good day. They will be impressed by your classy handling of their response. Meanwhile, you have left the door open for your calling them again in the future about a different product or service. Remember too, that every individual with whom you talk has a network of friends and contacts; you have a reputation to be concerned about. A prospect who says "Yes" tomorrow may be a friend of some-one who said "No" today.

DON'T LET A NEGATIVE CALL AFFECT YOUR NEXT ONE. You will have bad calls; that is, you will have calls where you are treated rudely. When you have such a call, shake it off; end the call politely, and take a couple of minutes to blow off steam before you jump back on the phone. Don't blame yourself for the other person's rudeness and incivility. You know very well that such individuals exist. If there's a window close to your desk (and if it's not dark and stormy outside), look out and say to yourself, "What a beautiful day!" Or think back to a really positive call you had a few minutes ago. In any case, keep the bad call in perspective, and don't let it affect your attitude on your next one.

CELEBRATE YOUR GOOD CALLS. It's important that when you have a really good call you take a couple of minutes to savor it. Share your success with a colleague or associate who is nearby. They will be glad for you and will themselves be buoyed by your success. Most importantly, realize in your own mind the significance of the good call. If your presentation works with one prospect, it will work with others! That's great news! Understand that you're **doing it right**! You can get back on the phone with a real charge of confidence.

CONVERT PROSPECTS TO CLIENTS. It is very important to follow-up with prospects who respond positively to your prospecting phone call. Do whatever it takes to make customers out of them. Send them product information in the mail along with a personal note that references your phone call; call them a second or third time. Make an appointment to see them personally. But by all means, don't lose a potential customer for lack of follow-up! Remember, you didn't do all that telephone prospecting just to let the fish that nibbled swim merrily away.

Qualifying Prospects

Strictly speaking, an individual is not a prospect until he has been qualified. Until you have determined that a person is ready, willing, and able to buy your product or service, he is actually just a name on a source list - only a **potential** prospect.

The prospecting phone call only **intends** to discover if an individual has an **interest** in your product or service, and, as a general rule, does **not** afford you an opportunity to qualify him. It is your very **first** contact with that person and **as such** must be handled with sensitivity and finesse. You can hardly ask specific qualifying questions of an individual whom you have just told that you are "not calling to sell anything." However, in the real world, it often happens that a prospecting call will **also** turn out to be a qualifying call. It is not uncommon for a person who expresses an interest in what you are selling to go on to reveal sufficient information about himself so that you can qualify him as a potential buyer right then and there.

Still, in most cases you will have to make a **second** call to an individual in order to qualify him as a prospect. And even on that second call you will not be able to employ a steam roller approach in order to get the qualifying information that you need, but you **will** have to maneuver the individual into a **straightforward** encounter with the product or service that you are selling so that the answers he gives to your qualifying questions will have a meaningful and concrete reference point. Or to say it more directly (and quite plainly!), it doesn't do any good to pussyfoot around with an individual and eventually discover that he is ready, willing, and able to buy something, if that **something** is not **precisely** the something that you are selling! If an individual has no real interest in what you are selling, the quicker you find it out, the better!

Once you have confirmed, however, that a person has a genuine interest in your product or service, you must qualify him on the basis of three criteria: (1) Readiness to buy, (2) Willingness to buy, and (3) Ability to buy.

QUALIFY FOR READINESS TO BUY. You must find out **when** an individual might buy your product. Is he ready to buy it immediately? Within 30 days? 60 days?

When? Depending on the product or service that you sell, there will be some **reasonable** period of time beyond which it is not practical for you to wait for a prospect to make the buy-decision. For most salespersons 90 days is the outside limit of the "suspense" period during which they are willing to make repeated contacts with a prospect to "get his business." The best way to find out when a prospect will be ready to buy is to **ask** him. For example: "How soon will you decide about this matter?" Or: "How much time will you need to decide about purchasing this product (or service)?" You have nothing to lose by being direct. You can only lose by allowing an individual who is not really serious about your product to string you along indefinitely before finally saying "No."

QUALIFY FOR WILLINGNESS TO BUY. You must find out if a person **desires** to buy what you are selling. Does he **want** it? Hopefully, by the time you qualify an individual for willingness, you will have already demonstrated that your product or service matches the needs that he has declared himself to have. Again, you can be very direct. You might summarize very briefly just **how** your product or service meets the particular needs which he has discussed with you and then ask directly: "Is this product something that you are willing to buy? Do you see it as something that will help your situation?"

QUALIFY FOR ABILITY TO BUY. Of course the most important qualifying question has to do with money. Does the individual have the financial resources to make the purchase that you are recommending? The cost of the product or service you are selling should not come as a surprise to the prospect. It should have been a part of the information which you disclosed to him prior to your formal qualifying effort. And, in fact, many prospects will themselves ask at an early point in their contact with a salesperson, "How much does this product (service) cost?" because they do not want to spend **their** time chasing after something they can't afford to buy. So the point is that most individuals who are still talking with you when you get around to asking if they have the necessary bucks **probably do**. Once again, ask the qualifying question directly. For example: "Will your cash flow accommodate this purchase comfortably?" Or: "Is the amount of this purchase something you want to handle with a single payment?"

Summary

It is obvious from the discussion in this chapter that prospecting and qualifying is a vital function for the successful salesperson. The most important thing to remember when you undertake this task is to **stay realistic**. Remember that it is **always** a percentage operation. Don't set unrealistic goals for yourself. Even if you are prospecting a source (prospect pool) that has strong potential, you should not expect to get a positive response of more than around 30 % at best. You don't have to bat "a thousand;" major leaguers are overjoyed to bat .300.

Prospecting and qualifying is an ongoing game for the professional salesperson; there's always tomorrow. See it as the game that it is. Expect a lot of noes, and don't be ruffled by them. Relatively speaking, a mere handful of yeses can make you rich, while all the noes in the world are like so much water off a duck's back. Keep a good attitude; know your business, and you'll "get the business!"

5

THE APPOINTMENT

Introduction

The appointment is something very special. Anyone who has done any cold-calling knows that. Anyone who has ever sold door-to-door knows it. Anyone who has broken a tooth on a weekend knows it! Without an appointment you're an intruder, an interrupter, a loose cannon posing a threat to another person's structured universe. In a word, **without an appointment**, you're not welcome!

But **with an appointment**, you're part of the home team. You're an invited guest. You're a visitor who is expected. You're on the prospect's schedule! If you're a salesperson with an appointment, you're halfway to the bank! That's how important an appointment is. Why is an appointment so important for a salesperson? Because it's more than an appointment; it's an invitation to you to make your sales presentation. For a salesperson, an appointment is not just an appointment; it's a sales interview!

Understanding the Importance of the "Four Basics"

So, if an appointment is so very important, you want to be certain that when you get one, you don't blow it. There are four messages - the **"Four Basics"** - that all effective salespersons **convey at every appointment**: (1) "I'm a good guy." (2) "I like and respect you." (3) "I know my business." (4) "I can save you money," "I can make you money," or "I have something that you need." If you are successful in delivering these four messages during an appointment with a prospect, the odds are very good that you will make a sale. Now let's examine these messages in detail.

1 - "I'M A GOOD GUY." On every appointment you need to remember that as a salesperson you are selling yourself as much as you are selling your product or service. Chances are that your prospects could buy a product similar to the one you are selling from any number of competitors. They will choose to buy your product only if they decide that they like you. If you are successful in selling yourself on an appointment, you probably will be successful in making a sale. One of your main objectives for an appointment must be to get your prospect to see that you are indeed a "good guy." You should present yourself to your prospect as the kind of person that he would see as a "best friend" - someone that he enjoys being with and talking to.

2 – "I LIKE AND RESPECT YOU." Everybody loves to be respected and well liked. Naturally, not all of your prospects will be equally likeable or deserving of respect, but each one will have positive traits and characteristics that you can focus upon. As a salesperson it is very important that you convey to your prospect the fact that you do like and respect him as a person. By thinking of him as a friend and not just a potential sale, it will be easy to send him the message that you respect his accomplishments in business and that you appreciate (if not admire) him as an individual.

3 – "I KNOW MY BUSINESS." ("And that includes **your** business!") If you can't convince a prospect that you are an expert in your own business and that you understand how your business can help **his** business, then you probably won't **get** much business! A prospect has the right to expect a salesperson to be a competent resource person and consultant with regard to the product or service that he is selling. You want to come across as a confident, informed person who has broad and cutting-edge knowledge of your product. If you truly are an expert in your own industry, you won't need to make any foolish attempts to impress a prospect with exaggerated and unbelievable claims for your product. Instead, you will be able to present yourself as an honest and expert business consultant who will be warmly received by the prospect.

4 – "I CAN SAVE YOU MONEY;" "I CAN MAKE YOU MONEY;" "I HAVE SOMETHING THAT CAN HELP YOU." No appointment will turn into a sale for you if you fail to achieve this fourth basic. You must give the prospect a reason for buying; you must create motivation for him. In business, motivation is a function of money - making money or saving money. In many cases, the product or service you are selling may save money (or make money) for the customer **indirectly**. For example, what you are selling may enable the customer's business to save time, reduce employee turnover, or decrease the amount of its required warehouse space, etc.

But whether you save the prospect money directly or indirectly does not matter; you are still increasing his profit, and that's what business is all about. So, get out your calculator, tell your prospect to grab a pencil and write down the numbers, add them up, and look at the bottom line. Whether you are selling a tangible or intangible product, you must show your prospect exactly how it will benefit him. **How it will benefit him** is his **motivation** for buying. By taking your product or service, relating it to your prospect's business, and demonstrating how it will work for him, you make it personal - something that the prospect will **want**, not just need.

How to Prepare Yourself for an Appointment

There are a number of things you should do before going to an appointment. Naturally, some appointments will require special preparation, but there are standard tasks that should be accomplished before any appointment.

POSITIVE MENTAL ATTITUDE. Experienced salespersons can usually take this psychological posture for granted. They learned early on that without it they couldn't survive in sales. But for many young and/or inexperienced salespeople, gearing up for an appointment is an ongoing challenge. There are several things that you can do to develop a positive outlook for an upcoming appointment.

Think about your personal ambiance. When you go to an appointment, you have an opportunity to showcase your personal ambiance. People talk about their favorite restaurant or hotel as having a certain ambiance - something that is difficult to describe or define - a very special, positive feeling or mood or tone. Well, people have an ambiance too, and there is no way that it can be fully communicated on the telephone. The appointment gives you an opportunity to project or radiate your personal ambiance, and that's a plus!

But, of course, you can't showcase something until you know what it is. So you must **think** about your personal ambiance and define it. It's all of your best qualities - the things about you that people like - your sense of humor, the intelligence that shows through your conversation, your playful self-deprecation that nobody can take seriously, your contagious laugh, your natural enthusiasm for and interest in just about everything, and many more things besides. You may be surprised to discover what an interesting person you are! The sales appointment will give you an opportunity to use that captivating person (you!) to your own advantage.

It's a common thing for a young salesperson to talk about how "relieved" he was when he discovered that the prospect he had driven to see was not in his office that day. You will **never** hear a sales rep who understands the value of his personal ambiance rejoicing that a prospect was out of his office when he called.

Be optimistic. All great salespeople are optimists, at least about their sales abilities. Too many people think that optimism is something that you have to get from "out there" - from outside yourself, and they wonder how they will ever "find" it. But there's nothing mysterious or ethereal about optimism. It comes from inside yourself; you can plant it and grow it. Optimism is just the natural outgrowth that comes from knowing all about the product or service that you sell, and believing in it. The only additional thing that's needed to make your optimism bear fruit is to find a prospect who needs your product or service so that you can tell him about it.

Everybody has bad days. If you have a day when you are really down, for whatever reason, cancel and reschedule your appointments. Prescription medications, personal tragedies - any number of things - can leave even the most "cockeyed optimist" thrown for a loop. So if, or when, this happens to you, give yourself a break and an opportunity to regroup before you hit the pavement again. Chances are that calling on prospects when you're battling a serious personal or medical problem would be counterproductive anyway.

Prep yourself on the way to an appointment. You're in your car and on your way to an appointment. What last-minute things can you do to insure that you will stay "up" until you meet your prospect? Some salespersons make tapes with their favorite motivational music and play them on the way to an appointment. The selections are your choice, of course. The music doesn't have to be trumpets and thunder like the theme song from "Rocky," but it probably shouldn't be "music to relax by."

Some individuals like to drive to an appointment in silence, taking the opportunity to run through a sort of mental countdown, reviewing what they know about the prospect, and taking one last walk through the sales presentation they plan to make. However you decide to spend these last minutes before an appointment, it probably is best not to surf the radio dial or play a cassette or disk that could detract from your focus.

PRODUCT INFORMATION. There's never an excuse for going to an appointment unprepared to answer questions about the product or service you are selling. The fact is that if you don't know the "story" on what you are selling, if you can't recite the features and benefits ("chapter and verse") of your product or service, you're not going to make a sale anyway; so you might just as well cancel the appointment. It's amazing that any salesperson ever fails to understand the importance of knowing product information forwards and backwards. There's no way you can go to an appointment with a confident attitude if you lack a thorough mastery of product information. And the bottom line, of course, is that there's no way that you can sell without it.

Sometimes at an appointment a prospect will ask a question about a related product or service - one that your company sells, but not the one you had prepped the prospect for. Or he may inquire about a competing product. In such cases you can simply say that you will be glad to check on whatever it is that he wants to know and get back to him with an answer in a day or so. Nobody can expect you to know everything about all of the products and services that are related to the one you have prepared yourself to sell on a particular day. But you should always try to anticipate questions about related or competing products so that you don't lose an opportunity to close a prospect on a first appointment.

PROSPECT INFORMATION. Usually, getting an appointment with a prospect is the result of more than one phone contact with the individual. That means that you have invested time in discovering and cultivating the prospect. No doubt you have qualified him to be sure that he is, in fact, a potential customer who needs and can afford to buy your product or service. But, most likely, you have dozens of other similar prospects. It is only natural, then, for a salesperson who is pressed for time (And what salesperson isn't?) to rush off to an appointment with a particular prospect without bothering to review all of the specific information that he has gathered on that individual. But that is a big mistake. Always review your notes on a prospect before going to an appointment with him. You may have some personal information that will help you establish rapport quickly, or you may have a note about his business or professional circumstances that will help you personalize the focus of your sales presentation.

CURRENT EVENTS INFORMATION. Every salesperson should keep up with the leading stories in national and world news as well as significant events taking place at the state and local levels. A prospect may have been reading a newspaper just before your arrival and may greet with you with a question like "Well, what do you think of what's happening with so and so, and blah blah blah?" He will not be impressed if you respond by saying, "Beats the heck out of me." Fishing around with current events items can often help you identify one or more of the prospect's "hot buttons" during the ice-breaking period at the beginning of the appointment.

PERSONAL APPEARANCE. For many salespersons personal appearance is not an issue that comes up every time they have an appointment. They adhere to a standard dress code that works for them day in and day out regardless of the particular prospects they might be seeing on any given day. But how does someone new to sales know how to dress, how to evaluate his personal appearance before going to an appointment? There are three guidelines to be considered here.

Imitate successful salespersons in your industry. An obvious and appropriate thing for a new salesperson to do is to pay attention to how successful salespersons in the industry dress. If you work out of an office which has several (or many) salespeople, notice how the most successful ones dress. Talk to them about their choice of clothes; they will be complimented that you regard their opinion as being important. When you call on prospects, you will doubtless see salespersons from competing companies; observe how they are dressed. They will not all look the same. Imitate the styles worn by the most professional and successful of your competitors.

Consider how your prospects will be dressed. Even if you are new to sales, you will quickly get a feel for how your prospects dress. Depending on the industry that you are a part of, your customers may dress very uniformly or not uniformly at all. As a general rule, you want to dress like your customers. If your prospects always wear suits, you should too. If most of your prospects and customers dress informally, that raises a question for you. You never want to be "less dressed" than the person you are calling on, but you don't want to be overdressed. On the other hand, many customers expect salespersons to be more "dressed up" than themselves. Being called on by someone in business attire (suit and tie, etc.) makes them feel important. If prospects and customers come to you, rather than you going to them, as in the case of the salesperson who works at an automobile dealership, then you should dress according to company policy or in the style of the most professional senior salespeople at the business.

Pay close attention to personal grooming. You should always be absolutely clean. Being an amateur gardener at home or a do-it-yourselfer around the house is no excuse for having paint or dirt on your hands or under your fingernails when you go to work and "meet the public." A really hot day is no excuse for a break in your deodorant protection. Your hair should never look like it was shampooed yesterday (or horror of horrors! the day **before** yesterday). Fingernails should be appropriately clipped and shaped, cuticles pushed back. Inappropriate facial hair (in or protruding from ears or nose, etc.) should be removed. Colognes and perfumes should never be offensive. Teeth should always be clean and breath fresh. Clothes should always be clean and wrinkle-free, shoes shined and polished. Remember, the customer or prospect who perceives you as being less than fastidious about **your** personal grooming is very likely to conclude that you might not be diligent about **his** business interests.

Listed below are some general rules that any salesperson can use to evaluate his personal appearance:

- Always avoid the outrageous or unusual in fashions and personal grooming.
- Don't wear gaudy or pretentious jewelry.
- Don't wear or carry superfluous accessories.
- Err on the side of the conservative rather than on the side of the flamboyant.
- Avoid having a "thrown together" look as if you ran out of time for dressing and grooming.

CLEAN CAR. Most salespeople don't think about their car as being something they have to be concerned about as they're preparing for an appointment, but you can never predict when a prospect or customer may decide to walk you to your car at the end of an appointment. Or, right in the middle of a sales interview that is moving along nicely a prospect may say, "Hey, let's take a lunch break; let's drive over to Davidson's. We'll finish talking about this deal over there!" There's always an outside chance that your prospect may see your car, even ride in it. So be prepared! It's an extension of you, so it must always look first-class, inside and out.

How to Present Yourself at an Appointment

When you go to an appointment, you want to be sure that you present yourself in the most positive way possible. Among the cliches that people in sales like to toss around is the one that says, "You never get a second chance to make a first impression," and of course there's truth in it. What you transmit (not just with your words, but with your **total presence**) to a prospect during the first few minutes of an appointment **is** very important. But, in fact, from the beginning to the end of every appointment you are communicating with your prospect on two different levels - nonverbal and verbal (visual and vocal).

NONVERBAL BEHAVIOR. Nonverbal behavior is visual behavior; it is what your prospect sees you do. It is your body's language, and it often takes precedence over the verbal message that you send with the words you speak.

Avoid sending conflicting messages. If a prospect thinks that your words are telling him something different than what your body is saying, he will question your verbal message, and you will lose credibility. You must never send conflicting messages. Your words must always be reinforced by the nonverbal signals you send.

> *Example:* Imagine introducing yourself to someone at a party. You reach out to shake hands, and the other person responds with outstretched hand saying, "Glad to meet you." But he avoids making eye contact, looking past you at someone who is standing behind you. Naturally, you doubt his verbal message because he has contradicted it with his visual behavior.

Send messages that reinforce each other. Reinforce your verbal message with body language that corroborates it. Use eye contact, facial expression, hand gestures, etc. to make your spoken message convincing.

> *Example:* Picture again the scenario cited in the example above, but this time the other person not only reaches out to shake your hand, but looks you directly in

the eye, smiles warmly, says "I'm really glad to meet you," and reaches out with his left hand to clasp your right shoulder. This time your reaction is warm and positive. The other person has communicated to you that he is genuinely pleased to meet you.

Establish good eye contact. It would be hard to overstate the importance of eye contact. There are all kinds of old sayings about the importance of it. Parents used to tell their children that if they didn't look an adult directly in the eye when speaking, the older person might think that they weren't telling the truth. Many people still believe that an individual's eyes reveal not only the degree of his sincerity, but the level of his intelligence. But conventional wisdom aside, good eye contact gives you credibility, or at least gains you the opportunity to earn it.

But there is another thing about the eyes. We take in the world with our eyes and ears. Our eyes aren't just public relations accessories for impressing other people - sending them messages about how warm and honest and intelligent we are. We use our eyes to satisfy our interest in and curiosity about other people and the world outside ourselves. We size up other persons with our eyes, just as they do us.

So, eye contact is very important at an appointment. When you walk into your prospect's office, establish it immediately, but don't freeze your eyes to his. Look at him overall, up and down, quietly taking his measure without being offensive. You want to appear to be interested in him, curious about his physical presence, but not judgmental. You need to remember during this time of first impressions that **you** are not the **only** person being scrutinized; your **prospect** is also "under the glass" - yours. But even as you are "deciding" about your prospect, he is making a judgment about you; within thirty seconds after meeting you, he will decide whether you are confident and secure or a frightened puppy. In large measure, his decision will be based on the eye contact that you have exchanged with him.

Use body language that says you are an interested listener. The successful salesperson knows that listening is an activity that yields double benefits. At the same time that he is gaining valuable information from his prospect, he is afforded the opportunity to send positive, point-winning messages to the speaker. Everybody likes to feel that what they say is important. A prospect is no exception to the rule. There are dozens of ways in which you can show that you are listening intently to your prospect - arching an eyebrow, tightening your lips, touching your chin, nodding your head, leaning on one elbow with hand under chin, straightening your shoulders, leaning forward in your chair, making a note to yourself, tilting your head, etc. Remember that a skillful listener is **sending** messages as well as receiving them.

Display positive overall body language. A judge at a livestock show is required to complete a checklist that assigns points to an animal in several different categories. Among them is one called "General Appearance." The judge must grade the animal on the basis of the overall impression that it makes upon him. Salespersons are also judged on the general impression that they make. A slouching, shuffling, fidgeting sales rep is not likely to score very high with most prospects.

Much has been written about the many facets of general body language; everything is important, from how you sit to how you communicate with different movements of the head. But the bottom line is that you should do those things that appear to be natural (rather than affected) and that give the impression that you are an enthusiastic and confident professional selling a product or service that will benefit the prospect in important ways.

VERBAL BEHAVIOR. Verbal behavior is vocal or spoken behavior. It is what your prospect **hears** you say; it is the words you speak. In the first two chapters of this book we addressed the importance of **how** you speak the words that you deliver to a prospect or customer, and at the beginning of this chapter we discussed at length the content of **what** you must communicate (the "Four Basics") to a prospect at an appointment. Suffice it to say at this point that when you present yourself and your product or service to a prospect, you must speak with energy and enthusiasm, avoiding anything whatsoever in your delivery that might be interpreted as tentativeness or uncertainty on your part about the product you are selling. The deliberateness of your straightforward presentation will engender confidence in the prospect.

How to Make an Appointment

THE APPOINTMENT-SETTING PHONE CALL. Appointments are usually made on the telephone. In most cases a salesperson will have talked to the prospect once or twice prior to making the appointment-setting call. Careful planning needs to go into this phone call since it should include the four elements discussed below.

Take control in the introductory segment. You should begin the phone call with a warm, friendly greeting in which you identify yourself, your product (or service), and your company. You want to help the prospect "make the connection" with you; you want him to **remember** your previous phone conversation. You also want to gain control of the call right at the beginning; you do not want to give him an opportunity to define you as an outsider - an intruder trying to sell him something. Of course, you **are** an outsider wanting to sell him something, but you have "paid dues" with him in a previous phone call (or calls); and now you want him to feel obligated to talk with you as a person who has at least **some** (never mind how **small** a claim) claim to his time and interest.

> *Example.* Bill Franklin, the president and CEO of a company that operates a fairly large manufacturing plant, receives a phone call from Doug Rockhurst, a sales representative for Workspace Engineering Systems, Inc. "Good morning, Bill. This is Doug Rockhurst with Workspace Engineering. You remember we talked the other day about the heating and air conditioning systems in your plant. We discussed the problem of seasonal heat and air loss and had just started to talk about your need for more light in certain work areas when you were called into a staff meeting. I promised I'd get back with you in a few days, and that's why I'm calling now."

> *Commentary on Example.* The salesperson in this example may be stretching the facts a bit by saying that he and the prospect "talked about" and "discussed" certain problem areas relating to the prospect's factory. In reality, the salesperson may have merely asked a couple of questions related to heating, air conditioning, and lighting in the prospect's plant without getting any real answers. And, in fact, he may suspect that there really wasn't any staff meeting the other day, but that Bill Franklin simply used that as an excuse for cutting off the phone call. So it may well be that the salesperson has only the tiniest, flimsiest claim on the prospect, but he calmly and smoothly (not to mention **boldly**) plays his deuce card as if it were an ace.

This is exactly what you must do in the first 2-3 minutes of the appointment setting phone call - stake out a claim to the prospect's time and interest. You *may* not get away with the kind of smooth boldness used by Doug Rockhurst in the example above, but you *just* might. You have nothing to lose by trying, and it would take a grumpy prospect indeed to respond to the polite but assertive Doug by saying, "I don't know *what* you're talking about; I don't remember talking about *anything* with you!" More likely, the plant owner will be somehow flattered by the salesman's persistent attention.

It takes a little imagination and a lot of guts to open an appointment-setting phone call by playing the role of a *hired consultant* when your only previous contact with the prospect was a brief phone call which you initiated and the prospect cut short. But this is just what Doug Rockhurst does, and it's *exactly* what you must do, too.

If in the introductory 2-3 minutes of this phone call you allow the prospect to take control by asking one of the following questions: (1) "Who **are** you?" (2) "Do I **know** you?" (3) "Have we spoken **before**?" or (4) "What are you **selling**?" you are all but officially dead. It will take a miracle, and more skill than you have demonstrated up to this point in the phone call, to salvage it. You have allowed the **prospect** to take **control** and define **you** as an outside **intruder** who is trying to **sell** him something.

Establish the need for the immediate purchase of your product or service. During the second 2-3 minutes of this phone call you must move quickly to lay out important reasons why the prospect should give prompt attention to his need for the product or service that you are selling. Review the "Four Basics" described at the beginning of this chapter and use the fourth one here - "I can save you money," "I can make you money," or "I have something that can help you." The example below continues on with the scenario of Doug Rockhurst, Workspace Engineering Systems sales rep and Bill Franklin, company president.

> *Example.* "Mr. Franklin, I wanted to get back with you promptly because we're only about six months away from the hottest part of the summer. I know that you must be dreading the power bills that you'll be getting when the air conditioning system in your plant has to be kept running 24 hours a day. We didn't have a chance to talk about the details of the heat and air loss at your factory the other day, but I took a few minutes on Monday to drive over there and gather enough information to allow me to run some tentative numbers for you. I'm certain now that I can save you some major dollars this summer." (Intentional pause.)
>
> Bill Franklin interrupts Doug Rockhurst's pause by saying, "What do you mean, you gathered information? How could you run any numbers?"
>
> Doug jumps in quickly with his reply: "Well, I stepped off the dimensions of your building and figured the square footage of air conditioned space. Then, taking into account the fact that your plant has no insulation materials in place and that its 240 windows are of the old non-thermal type, I calculated the BTU's of air conditioning that would be required to cool your plant

during the hottest summer months. Then, I ran a second calculation based on the amount of air conditioning that would be required for your plant if Workspace Engineering installed the appropriate amount of insulation material and replaced your old windows with new ones of the thermal type. The air loss you're presently experiencing could be greatly reduced. In fact, my estimate is that with the building modifications I'm recommending, you could save at least $86,000 this summer in air conditioning cost. Of course that says nothing of the savings you could effect next winter during the several months that you have your heating system on line."

Commentary on Example. The Workspace Engineering Systems rep has taken the bull by the horns here. He has definitely gained control of the conversation, not just by what he is **saying**, but by what he has **done**. After an initial phone call to the plant's president - a phone call that was cut short by the prospect - Doug became proactive, did some strategic homework, went back to the phone, and put the ball smack in the middle of his prospect's court. He has certainly succeeded in getting Bill Franklin to see the need for immediate action with regard to making a decision about what he is selling-namely, workspace environmental systems.

Match your product's (or service's) features to the needs of the prospect. In the third 2-3 minute segment of the appointment-setting phone call you must make the prospect see that the specific **features** of your product or service match his specific **needs**. The example below is a continuation of the scenario which we have been following.

Example. "I will need to do an inside inspection of your building to come up with exact figures for the heat and air loss that you're experiencing during the winter and summer seasons. Frankly, though, I'm sure that carrying out the plant modification that I am proposing will save you as much money on your **heating** bill in the winter as it does on your **cooling** bill in the summer. Your savings on an annual basis will very likely approach $200,000. And besides that, the design of the replacement thermal windows which Workspace Engineering will install will give you a lot more **light** in the work areas of your building. I would estimate about 20% more; I can give you an exact number after I've made the inside inspection of your facility."

Commentary on Example. Doug, clearly in charge of the phone conversation now, sails through the third segment of the call, explaining for the company president how the plant modification carried out by Workspace Engineering will save him major dollars and provide better lighting for his workers.

Set the appointment. The final segment of the appointment-setting phone call offers little challenge to the salesperson who has successfully accomplished the three segments which preceded it. All that remains to be done is to actually set the appointment with the prospect. The important thing to remember at this point is that you must retain control of the conversation. Don't **ask** for an appointment, allow the prospect a small latitude of choice as to the **time** of your meeting with him, but take for granted that the appointment will occur. You are merely being considerate to allow the prospect to "fill in the blank" as to **when**. The example below continues the story of Doug Rockhurst and Bill Franklin.

Example. "Listen, Bill, I feel like this has been a really productive conversation, but I've got to keep an appointment with a customer here at the office. We need to get together real soon so that I can fine-tune those numbers for you and enable you to make a decision in time to save some serious money this summer. I'm going to be up on the north side of the city on Friday. How about if we get together sometime in the afternoon? What time will work for you?"

Commentary on Example. Bill Franklin will find time to see Doug Rockhurst on Friday afternoon. He will see him because the Workspace Engineering rep has successfully communicated to him the final element of the "Four Basics" discussed at the beginning of this chapter - "I can save you money; I can help you." Notice how Doug is **closing** Bill even as he sets the appointment time. Doug tells him that he wants to put him in a position that will allow him to "make a decision in time to save some serious money this summer."

So, we have examined the four parts of the appointment-setting phone call:

- Take control in the introductory segment.
- Establish the need for the immediate purchase of your product or service.
- Match your product's (or service's) features to the needs of the prospect.
- Set the appointment.

The Actual Appointment - Phase One

ARRIVE 5 MINUTES EARLY. Always show up for an appointment exactly five minutes early. If you are consistent in doing this, you will program your prospects and customers to expect you five minutes before the appointment time. They will see you as being extremely punctual, and you will gain a subtle advantage of power and control. They will feel ever so slightly **pushed** by you, though in an acceptable way; for you will appear as simply being highly dependable and responsible.

DON'T SIT IN THE LOBBY. You will often find yourself in a lobby or reception area waiting to see a prospect with whom you have an appointment. Most people who are waiting to see another person sit down to wait. This is a mistake. It puts you in a passive role. Without realizing it, and without intending to do it, you forfeit your power and independence to the secretary or receptionist, and indirectly to the prospect whom you have come to see.

Doubtless, when you arrive for an appointment, the receptionist will ask you to "Please have a seat until Mr. So-and-so can see you." Just thank the individual for his attention without explaining why you prefer **not** to sit while waiting for your prospect. Of course **you** understand fully why you want to be standing when Mr. So-and-so comes to the lobby to invite you back to his office. You do not want to be playing the role of a well-trained dog who has been taught to "Sit - Stay!" when you meet your prospect for the first time.

ANALYZE THE LOBBY. It is not unusual to have to wait several minutes before seeing a prospect. You should take advantage of this situation by using your time productively. You should analyze the lobby of your prospect's business office. By doing this you can often gain considerable information about the prospect himself as well as the business he operates. Think of yourself as a detective trying to deduce from the physical environment in which you find yourself as much as possible about the individual who conducts his business in this place. Remember, the more you know about your prospect, the more advantage you will have in the sales interview. The following questions will help you focus on the kinds of things you should observe.

- Is this environment professional or unprofessional?
- Is it clean or dirty?
- Is the flow of telephone and human activity slow, moderate, or intense?
- Does the reception area reflect organization and control or disorder and chaos?
- Do you see any objects that may reflect personal interests of your prospect?
- Are trophies on display? Are they company or personal trophies?
- If there are trophies, what activities do they represent?
- Do you see pictures or paintings on the walls? What do they tell you?
- What is your overall impression of the office (what you can see of it)?
- Is it upscale or modest?
- What type of office equipment do you see?
- Is this a high-tech office operation (computers, fax machines, etc.)?
- How are the employees dressed?
- Are there customers in the lobby? How are they dressed?
- What kind of language do you hear, cultivated or coarse?
- Do the employees appear to be well educated and sophisticated?
- Do you see business, professional, or fraternal signs or plaques in the lobby?
- What type magazines or newspapers are in the lobby?
- Do you see any evidence of religious or political affiliations?
- Is the decor of the lobby formal or informal?

DON'T WAIT MORE THAN 15 MINUTES. As a salesperson you must always guard against being put in a subservient position. If you arrive for an appointment 5 minutes ahead of the scheduled time and then wait 15 minutes, you have generously given your prospect 20 minutes to "catch up" or attend to whatever his problem may be. That is time enough! To wait longer than 20 minutes is to allow yourself to be treated rudely and without respect. The salesperson who waits passively for 50 minutes to see a prospect and then accepts a perfunctory "Sorry to keep you waiting" by responding with a smile and a cheerful "No problem" has forfeited any possibility of controlling the sales interview.

At the end of 15 minutes after your scheduled appointment time, walk calmly to the receptionist's desk, hand the individual one of your business cards and say, "I have a very busy day with several more appointments to keep. I cannot wait any longer. Please tell Mr. So-and-so that I will call him tomorrow." By taking this action you regain control from your prospect. If he is the least bit sophisticated and sensitive, he will apologize when you call the next day and will very likely appear punctually for your rescheduled appointment.

There are, of course, incorrigible jerks in this world; and you will encounter your share of them over time. They will be angered if you leave their business without seeing them, no matter how long you waited. But you will have lost nothing by leaving, and by so doing you will be able to keep **other** more productive appointments. If you have no other appointments for the day, at least you will have freed yourself to spend time prospecting for individuals of a higher caliber than the one whose office you left.

INITIATE THE INTRODUCTION WITH THE PROSPECT. You should already be standing when your prospect enters the lobby or reception area. Be alert and see him the moment he appears. Greet him by name, first and last, followed by your own name and a short greeting (e.g., "George Johnson; Robert Knight. Good to meet you.") Walk toward him and extend your hand as you greet him. Establish solid eye contact, and give him a warm smile and a firm handshake as you introduce yourself. (Avoid alarming him with a death-stare look or a vise- grip handshake.) By taking this initiative you will preempt his taking control of the situation even though you are on his turf.

BREAK THE ICE. As you walk with the prospect from the lobby to his office, start a casual conversation with him. You should have gathered enough information from your analysis of the reception area to enable you to throw out an observation or two along with a question that will "get him going."

> ***Example:*** "I couldn't help admiring the mounted Blue
> Marlin in the lobby; it's one of the biggest I've seen. Is it
> one that you caught?"

The idea here is to avoid walking in silence from the lobby to the prospect's office. Once again, by taking the initiative you have dodged being put into the passive role of a salesperson following quietly along behind the prospect. At the same time, you have taken the positive step of establishing yourself as a sensitive and interesting human being with the prospect.

This particular task ("Break the ice."), along with the next one ("Analyze the prospect's office.") discussed immediately below, should communicate to the prospect the first two elements of the "Four Basics" covered at the beginning of this chapter, namely, (1) "I'm a good guy" and (2) "I like and respect you."

ANALYZE THE PROSPECT'S OFFICE. After you have entered the prospect's office, continue the non-business conversation that you have already started. As you are talking (and listening!), look around to see if there is anything that will give you a clue as to the prospect's personal interests or hobbies. Move the conversation to focus on an object that you suspect reveals something significant about the prospect. Don't be afraid to walk over and look closely at a picture or an object that you are talking about. He will appreciate your interest in things that are meaningful to him. What you are doing here is establishing rapport at the social level. It is a very important task that, if accomplished, can lead to personal friendship, which is a great base upon which to build a business relationship.

MAKE THE TRANSITION FROM SOCIAL TO BUSINESS CONVERSATION. Making a smooth transition from personal to business talk is very important. This is a transition that you must make. If you ramble on too long chatting about personal things, you run the risk of creating a situation in which the **prospect** may take control of the conversation and make the transition to the discussion of the business at hand. **Never** allow this to happen. You certainly don't want the prospect to see you as a salesperson who "has time to kill;" nor do you want him to gain control of the sales interview by allowing him to determine its focus and flow.

There are all kinds of ways to manage the transition from social to business conversation. Many of the best ones are fairly direct. Three examples are listed below:

> *Example:* "I'm really glad you took time out of your busy day to see me. I have some exciting things to go over with you."

> *Example:* "I've been looking forward to meeting you since we spoke on the phone last week. You asked several questions about the service that my company provides. I think I can answer them best in person."

> *Example:* "Well, (pause) this has **really** been interesting conversation. I wish we could continue it, but I know we both have tough schedules for the rest of the day. So I guess we'd better get on with the show (brief pause). I brought this data sheet to show you the numbers that we ...."

Most experienced salespersons are very smooth at making this transition and handle it with such finesse that they are able to move a prospect from the social to the business stage of the sales interview with a very positive and open attitude.

The Actual Appointment - Phase Two

The tasks accomplished in this second phase of the actual appointment should communicate to the prospect the second two elements of the "Four Basics" discussed at the beginning of this chapter, namely, (1) "I know my business" and (2)

"I can save you money," "I can make you money," or "I have something that can help you."

MAKE THE SALES PRESENTATION. Too many salespersons virtually memorize a sales presentation and then at an appointment **tell** it to the prospect. But the best sales presentation in the world will probably not produce a sale if you do not relate whatever it is you are selling to the **needs** of the prospect. This means that you can't just rush into your sales pitch without making an effort to discover how your prospect's needs relate to the product or service you are selling.

If you have qualified the prospect prior to your appointment, you will already know **some** of his needs, but you should ask pointed questions in order to gain a fuller understanding of precisely what he is looking for. Then you should tailor your sales presentation in a way that enables you to show him exactly how certain features of your product or service will satisfy the very needs he has identified.

Depending on what you are selling, you may have to **create** a need for the prospect. For example, if you are selling a luxury product or service that individuals or businesses can easily get along without, then you will have to provide them with a motive for buying. You may have to appeal to their pride, social status, artistic sensitivity, etc. The personal knowledge that you are able to gain about a prospect will help you decide what type of appeal will be effective.

SELL AFTER-THE-SALE SERVICE. Explain to your prospect exactly what you are going to do for him after the sale takes place. Every potential customer needs assurance that your relationship with him is just beginning with the sale, not ending. Tell him that you are looking forward to a long-term relationship that will benefit you both, and that you understand that providing him with good service will be the key to your doing future business with him. Ask him directly if he has any questions about the service that he hopes to receive from you and your company. Selling after-the-sale service is doing troubleshooting in advance, before the fact; but it also increases the prospect's confidence in you and prepares him for the close.

CLOSE THE PROSPECT. An entire chapter (#7) in this book is devoted to the art of closing, but a reminder about the importance of asking a prospect for his business must be included here. By the time you see a prospect on an appointment, you have invested a substantial amount of time in your effort to win his business. You prospected and qualified him on the phone. You probably made a follow-up call, and you certainly made an appointment-setting call. Then you spent time preparing for and driving to the appointment. Obviously then, now that you are **at** the appointment establishing personal rapport with him and making your sales presentation, you don't want to pass up an excellent opportunity to close him. You

may not get the business on your first appointment, but that is why you set up the appointment in the first place. You **certainly** will not get it if you don't ask for it. So, ask!

He may raise one or more objections (See "Chapter 6"). If he does, answer them and close him again. Tell yourself that the **next** appointment you have with this individual will be for the purpose of selling **additional** business, not making an initial sale. Remember, business that's "all but closed" can't be taken to the bank. The sooner you close a sale, the sooner it appears in your paycheck.

ASK FOR REFERRALS. Whether or not you are able to close a prospect on a first appointment, you should have made a strong and positive impression on him. He should now perceive you as a knowledgeable professional who is selling a valuable product or service. You have created a perfect environment for asking him for referrals. There is every likelihood that he has associates and friends who are potential customers for the product or service that you are selling. Take him into your confidence; treat him as a professional consultant, and ask him directly if he can give you the names of qualified prospects who could benefit from your product or service. You will be surprised at what an effective method this is for adding to your list of prospects.

END THE APPOINTMENT IN A POSITIVE MANNER. As a professional salesperson, it is important that you always conduct yourself in a poised and positive manner. Even if you are terribly disappointed in the outcome of an appointment, you have nothing to gain by revealing your negative emotions. You have a professional image and reputation to uphold, and you cannot predict what the future may hold with regard to your relationship with this particular individual. Many a salesperson has lived to regret "burning a bridge" with a prospect who "acted like a jerk" at a first appointment.

You should end every appointment exuding confidence and enthusiasm whether it has been successful or not. After a few moments of casual conversation, stand up, reach out across the prospect's desk and shake hands. Thank him for his time and assure him that you look forward to seeing him again in the near future. Be as warm and friendly and upbeat as you were at the beginning of the appointment. Of course it is easy to be upbeat if you just made a sale, but remember that the true professional is undaunted by momentary rejections or setbacks. They are like a sneeze in a dust storm; they are not long-term allergies.

COLD-CALL NEXT DOOR. Before you drive away from your appointment, go next door and cold-call the business there. You have a "natural" introduction for yourself. You can say, "I was doing business next door with Mr. So-and-so, and since I was right here in your block I thought I should check with you to tell you about our

......" It's just possible that your product or service is the very thing that the business next door needs, or is actually **looking** for. You have just given your sales presentation at your appointment, so it's fresh in your mind. What's to be lost by playing it one more time right next door. If it turns out that your timing is bad for the business next door, qualify the owner as a prospect and make an appointment for another day. Always checking next door when you're out on an appointment is a great way to prospect in person without going out of your way to do so.

Summary

We have covered a great deal of very important material in this chapter. It is probably fair to say that this present chapter taken along with the two chapters that follow it ("Handling Objections" and "Closing") is the very *heart* of this book on professional selling. Just below is a checklist of the topics (concepts and techniques) that we've discussed. Study the list carefully, and if there are any topics that you feel uncomfortable about, go back and read them again. There is nothing in this chapter that you can't do! It's all just a matter of *knowing* what's to be done and gaining experience in *doing* it.

- Understanding the **Four Basics**. *Connecting* with your prospect.
- Preparing yourself for an appointment. Getting *ready*.
- Presenting yourself at an appointment. *Doing* it.
- Making an appointment. *Gaining* the prospect's interest.
- Performing at the appointment. *Getting* the business!

6

HANDLING OBJECTIONS

Introduction

WHAT IS AN OBJECTION? It is exactly what the term implies. It is a prospective customer's objecting to something about the proposed product or service being offered. It is the prospect's giving voice to resistance to some aspect of the sales proposal being made. To many salespersons an objection is something horrible, something dismal and defeating. It is the wrench that has been thrown in the cogs of a smooth-rolling sales presentation. To some salespersons an objection is the end of their control of the interview with the potential customer.

But what **should** an objection be to the well-trained and experienced salesperson? An opportunity to shine. An invitation to move the sales presentation boldly and effectively forward. An opportunity to create an environment for closing the prospect. How so? A customer who raises an objection is listening; a client who objects is engaged - connected to the sales presentation - perhaps negatively, but nonetheless connected. This is a plus!

STEP UP TO THE PLATE! What should be **done** with an objection when one comes your way? Slap it over the right field fence for a home run! Absolutely! Can you imagine a great baseball hitter dreading his turn at bat? A great shortstop fearing that a hot ground ball will be hit to him? Never! Great hitters **live** for their time at the plate; great shortstops **dream** of charging hot smashes on the ground. Great salespersons see objections in just this way. Objections give them the opportunity to **perform**, decisively and powerfully!

Why do strong salespersons take such a positive outlook on objections? Because they have prepared themselves. Because they are ready. Because they have "shown up for the game on time," and have "come dressed to play!" How do they do this? How do they accomplish it? They accomplish it by having a positive mental attitude.

Positive Mental Attitude

THE "THREE MUST'S." There are three elements that are absolutely essential to a salesperson's achieving a positive mental attitude.

1 - UNDERSTAND YOUR PRODUCT OR SERVICE. Do your homework, gathering facts and figures that prove the worth of the product or service that you are marketing. Examine all of the reasonable objections that could be raised against it and satisfy yourself that they don't "stand up." Thus you can make a rational (intellectual) decision that what you are selling has real value, and that buyers will benefit significantly from it.

2 - BELIEVE IN YOUR PRODUCT OR SERVICE. Internalize the rational research that you have done in ways that make you a personal advocate for the product or service that you are selling. Your advocacy will be rooted in personal commitment (**faith** in the product or service) and will take on ethical and emotional dimensions.

3 - KNOW THAT YOU ARE NOT ALONE. Develop the sense of belonging to a **team**. You will be buoyed up by your awareness that you have colleagues and satisfied customers who believe in what they are selling and what they have bought.

DEADLY CONSEQUENCES OF NOT ACHIEVING THE "THREE MUSTS." It may be belaboring the obvious to point out how important it is for a salesperson to **avoid** the **converse of these three rules**. Nonetheless, the consequences of an individual "doing the opposite" of these rules are too serious to pass over.

1 - NOT UNDERSTANDING THE PRODUCT or service you are selling is the kiss of death. You can never feel secure or confident if you don't understand the strengths and benefits of what you are selling. A great public speaker was once asked if she could imagine any situation which would cause her to have stage fright. Her answer was: "Only if I were asked to speak about something I know nothing about."

2 - NOT BELIEVING IN THE PRODUCT or service you are selling is like sitting down at a table to eat something that you have a strong distaste for. You will not eat with gusto; you will not stay at the table very long; you will leave the table frustrated and with a bad taste in your mouth. It is a rare thing to find a successful salesperson who is selling something he doesn't believe in.

3 - NOT SEEING YOURSELF AS PART OF A TEAM made up of successful salespeople and satisfied customers condemns you to perceiving yourself as an isolated swimmer battling the force of an opposing tide. Avoid (like the plague!) associates who are consistently pessimistic, cynical, and discouraged. Negativism, like rust, spreads out and taints whatever (whoever) is close to it.

Steps for Handling an Objection

Now that we have seen how the successful salesperson achieves and maintains a strong, positive attitude, let's examine exactly how, with this positive outlook in hand, he performs in the face of an objection. The answer should be: logically and intelligently.

THE FOUR STEPS. Sales manuals have traditionally described three steps for handling an objection - (1) pause, (2) agree, and (3) overcome. We are adding a fourth step here to this procedure and changing the names slightly in the interest of clarity.

1 - RECOGNIZE IT! Be constantly alert when your prospect is talking. Expect to hear an objection. Understand that you're hearing an objection when your prospect begins to voice one. Crank up your concentration level several notches. It is very important to hear **all** of an objection. You don't want to miss the beginning (first part) of the objection. You want to be able to look back and recall the context out of which the objection emerged.

2 - LISTEN TO IT! Understand it. Focus on what your customer is saying, not on how you are going to respond. Never interrupt your client. Resist the urge to "butt in" and explain away the objection before the prospect has finished stating it. Try to identify with your client in order to better understand the objection. **Look** like you're listening; your non-verbal body language should tell your client that you are **seriously** listening.

3 - DEFINE IT! Articulate it. Make sure your client sees that you have heard what he is saying. Call the objection by its "right name" ("a question about **risk**" or "a question about **return** on investment," etc. - whatever it is), and make sure that your prospect agrees that you have described and defined the objection accurately. You should actually begin your statement with words like, "I hear what you are saying.... You're concerned about....." Be sure to use some of the exact words and phrases used by your client. In addition, use a few technical or "trade" terms in your restatement of the objection. By using the professional language of your "industry," you will be communicating to the prospect that you fully understand the objection **and** that this is not the first time you have considered it. You should end your restatement of the objection with words like, "...and if that were the case ("...if that were to happen..." etc.), I can understand why you would be concerned."

This third step in handling an objection is the **confirmation** stage. You are telling your client that you accept the objection as something that is real (and valid) to him. By doing this you are not "giving away the company store;" you are simply confirming the prospect's right to make the objection. This step in handling an objection is of critical importance because it can establish credibility for you as a salesperson. It gives you the opportunity to be perceived as listening, reasoning, and helping rather than as pushing, telling, and selling. In a word, it can open up the whole sales interview, creating a climate in which easy interaction can occur.

4 - OVERCOME IT! If the objection is a serious one, it must be overcome. Use facts and figures to demonstrate decisively that your product or service (whatever you are selling) cannot reasonably be objected to on the ground(s) that your client has just used. You may be able to accomplish this in only a preliminary way in the live interview (orally), but you can promise to provide much more detail (facts and figures) in a written response that you will prepare at your earliest opportunity.

CONCLUSIONS. An important point to remember here is that most objections are rooted in a particular **perspective**. For example, a prospect may think that your product is too expensive. You can point out that initial-cost is only one part of the total picture. Long-term cost must be considered also; your product may have great durability, low maintenance-cost, high trade-in value, etc., etc. Or, perhaps your product has a higher initial-cost than that of a competitor, but the "service" which your company provides is superior to that provided by your competitor.

Overcoming an objection is mainly a matter of providing the customer with information that enables him to see that his objection evaporates in the context of the "total picture." This positive outcome is managed by the skillful salesperson's manipulation of the perspective from which the client's objection is viewed. In cases where the objection cannot be made to evaporate, the salesperson must come up with a trade-off that compensates for the valid objection. The trade-off may be **other** strengths of the product or service being sold, or it may be "something extra" such as high-quality customer service promised by the sales rep himself.

Standard Objections

All experienced salespeople know that there is at least a baker's dozen of common objections that come up again and again. Let's look now at some of the most important of these generic objections.

1 - COLD "NO." We call this objection the Cold "No" because the prospect gives no reason for objecting to the close that has been proposed. His response is just (only, simply) "No." Of course the prospect probably has a reason (perhaps more than one) for saying "No," but for whatever cause(s), he simply doesn't choose to explain his rejection of the proposal at hand.

We can better understand this objection if we think about another situation in life where the Cold "No" is used. Consider the parent-child situation in which a young child is begging a parent for permission to go next door to play with a friend. There may be a half dozen reasons why the parent denies the youngster's request, but past experience has taught the parent that it is useless to give the child a reason why he cannot go to play with his friend. A logical reason (or even several) will not put an end to the child's demand to go next door. In fact, giving a reason will probably prompt the child to argue against the reason, thus extending the duration of the conflict. So, the wise parent responds to the child's "Why?" by saying that there is no reason. The answer is simply, "No."

Many prospects are like the parent just described. They are seasoned veterans when it comes to hearing sales presentations. Experience has taught them that the quickest and easiest way out is to use the Cold "No." The inexperienced or timid salesperson at this point may find himself dismissed and out the door with plenty of time to ponder just what it was that he did wrong. The skillful salesperson, however, will not be caught flat-footed by this non-substantive objection and will insist on an explanation (a "why") from the prospect. The salesperson might say something like, "I know that my product (service) has features that would provide real benefits for you, so I must have failed somehow to communicate them to you. Why is it, exactly, that you are convinced that my product would not provide you with real advantages?" This type of direct question may gain from the potential customer the kind of specific response that will allow the salesperson to move once more to a close.

Some prospects, however, will resist the skillful questioning of even the most insistent and engaging salespersons. In such cases the thing to do is punt, that is, change the subject. Engage the prospect at the **interpersonal** level, rather than at the **product** level. Talk about things that the client can agree with. Create a "yes" atmosphere for a few minutes, and then with great poise and finesse say something like, "Gee, this is really interesting! We could talk about this for a **while**! But I've got more appointments, and I know that **you** are very busy. Let me try to summarize for you what I see as the most significant benefits of my product (service) for your operation here." Make no reference to the Cold "No" encountered previously; move forward smoothly and boldly to a new close. The worst you should get is a substantive objection which you can answer on the spot or, worst case, use as an invitation for a future sales interview to which you promise to bring considerable evidence to put to rest the objection that has been brought forward.

2 – "I WANT TO THINK ABOUT IT." This objection is one of the most common encountered by salespeople. Obviously, it has to do with timing. The prospect is wanting to put off making a decision about buying the product or service being offered. You need to remember that the customer may not use the "think about it" words; he may say something like the following:

- "I'm too busy right now."
- "I need to talk to my wife (or husband)."
- "I need to consult with my accountant."
- "I need to see how much money I have available right now."
- "Let me think about it overnight."

The intelligent salesperson needs to think through this objection. In the vast majority of situations the prospect is not stalling just for the heck of it, just to frustrate the salesperson. The potential customer is not putting off a decision just to guarantee himself the joy of having a second or third return call (or visit) from the salesperson! No. The prospect has a reason for stalling. You must discover what it is in order to move effectively ahead with the sales interview. There are several possibilities here; some of the most likely are:

- The prospect doesn't trust you.
- The prospect isn't sold on the value/benefits of the product/service.
- The prospect is already getting the product/service from another source.
- The prospect lacks the money to make the purchase immediately.

There are other possibilities that may explain the prospective customer's reluctance to make an immediate buy-decision, but the four named above are perhaps the most common. The skillful sales rep will not settle for the prospect's "I want to think about it" explanation; instead he will probe to discover what the **real** cause of the prospect's hesitancy is and then deal with it directly.

In the rare event that the customer is not hiding a serious reason for putting off a buy-decision, the sales rep must then create a climate for moving the prospect to immediate action. One way to create a sense of urgency is to demonstrate to the customer how he will **gain** by making an immediate decision. Show him that there is a monetary (or service) gain to be had by making the purchase now. There is also persuasive power in demonstrating the converse - namely, that failure to buy now will result in a real loss of profit, service, opportunity, etc.

A second method of moving a prospect to immediate action is to "play" on the busy-ness of your own schedule. This is a very delicate matter. Regardless of how busy you actually are, the prospect is likely to think that it is your duty to see him as many times as it may take for him to come to a comfortable decision about buying your product or service. What you want to communicate to the prospective customer is that you

- have a very successful business with many satisfied clients.
- have an extremely demanding schedule which makes follow-up calls difficult and costly for you to schedule.
- still want to satisfy fully his particular needs (questions, concerns, etc.).

If you have been skillful enough in creating a climate of urgency, and if the prospect really does **not** have a hidden reason for stalling, then you may be fortunate enough to hear him say, "Hey, I know you really are super busy, and what you've told me here makes sense to me; let's go ahead and do it right now!"

On the other hand, if the prospect still insists on "thinking about it," then you must nail down a specific time for a follow-up phone call or personal visit. Don't settle for anything as vague or amorphous as, "Well, I'll call you later" or "Well, OK, we'll talk again later." If you weren't successful in closing for the business, then at the very least you must be successful in closing for a second sales call.

3 – "I KNOW MORE THAN YOU." OR "I DON'T NEED YOU." When a prospect is satisfied with a product or service that he has already bought (or is about to buy), he often uses this objection. He may say something like:

- "I'm really very satisfied with the group insurance we already have."
- "I'm already taken care of in this area."
- "I don't think your product (service) is just what I'm looking for."
- "After reviewing all the facts, I've decided to go with Company X's product."
- "I already have a broker, and I'm happy with him."

In this situation the prospect most likely wants to dismiss you because he's satisfied with the product or service (comparable to yours) that he's already using. It is very important to discover **why** he is satisfied before trying to move your sales presentation forward.

- Is it a matter of product differentiation? Does he think there is none? Does he think that all products (or services) of this type are the same?
- Does he have a close relationship with the sales rep from whom he is buying the product or service he is currently using?
- Does he actually believe that the product (or service) that he is presently using is of superior quality, or a better buy, than the one you are selling?

You must probe in order to define for yourself precisely what sort of situation you are facing. Once you know, you must offer the prospect something **extra** that he is not receiving from his present supplier. You must provide him with an incentive for switching to your product. It may be a savings in dollars (cost); it may be the providing of improved service (better delivery time, better maintenance, etc.); or it may be the supplying of a superior product (more versatile, more durable, more profitable, etc.). Whatever the **extra** thing(s) is that you offer, it must be substantial enough to give the prospect a reason for doing business with you. The following bit of dialog demonstrates the kind of situation we have been describing here.

> *Example:*
> Prospect: I appreciate the time you've taken to give me this sales presentation, but I already have a stock broker that I'm quite satisfied with.
>
> Broker: That's fine, Mr. Jones. Many of my clients work with several different brokers because each one has expertise in a particular area. Generally speaking, most brokers aren't specialists in **all** areas of investing. I'm not interested in taking your account away from your other broker. I just want to review your present investment portfolio to see if I can discover any areas that may need some attention. My own investment speciality is retirement planning. What sort of financial program do you have in place for **your** retirement?

Notice that in this scenario the broker does not badmouth the prospect's present financial advisor. Instead, he suggests something special (something **extra**) that he can offer to the prospect. That is the strategy that must be used to overcome this objection. The prospect must be sold on the idea that he **does** need you and your product or service. He must be convinced that whatever his own area(s) of expertise may be, he can still profit from the expertise that you possess. In a word, he does **not** know more than you about the product you are selling.

4 – "I KNOW THAT I NEED IT, BUT...." This objection is very different, yet similar, to the objection just discussed (#3 above). In that objection, for all practical purposes, the prospect tells the sales rep, "I know more than you. I know what I need; I've already selected it. I have it now, so I don't need you." In this objection, the prospect admits that he **needs** your product or service (very different from #3), but balks at making the buy-decision (very similar to #3). All things considered, this objection should be easier to deal with. When a prospect admits that he needs your product, you should be more than half way to the bank!

In order to get a feel for this objection, consider the following statements made by prospects who use it:

- "I know I need a new car, but I'm not sure if it should be this **kind**."

- "I'd like to invest in a tax-free bond, but I'm uncertain about the interest-rate outlook for the future."

- "I want to buy the additional forty acres, but I'm not sure if I can afford the financing."

- "I like your prices, but I've been using Acme's products for so long that I'm not sure I want to make a change."

- "I know that I have to make a decision soon about our company's retirement program, but I haven't had time to make a comparative study yet."

The great thing about this objection, from the standpoint of the salesperson, is that the prospect **tells** you what his problem is! Solve his problem and you've got his business! The following scenario shows you how.

Example:

Textbook Sales Rep: So, it seems like you really do want to move to a more current textbook - one that teaches students about the many computer applications used by contemporary accounting firms.

College Professor: Yes, I do. But the problem is that accounting is a very numeric discipline, and I have a file cabinet full of practice exercises and tests that I've developed over several years; and they were **all** designed to mesh with the textbook I've been using for the last six years. If I were to change texts now, I would have hundreds of hours of work to do all over again!

Textbook Sales Rep: I can certainly understand your concern about that! That's why our editors and authors have developed a "Study Guide" to accompany our new accounting text. It contains hundreds of practice exercises and tests for students to use as they work through each chapter of the textbook. In addition, there's a Test Bank for the instructor which provides multiple exams for each chapter of the text.

College Professor: That sounds like a good start, but I'd still have to work out all the answers to the exercises and exams. I just don't have that kind of time.

Textbook Sales Rep: You're in luck, Professor Smithson. My company knows that most teachers these days have very little time to spend working out problems. That's the kind of "busy work" you just don't have time for. So we developed an Instructor's Manual that has all of the answers for the exercises, practice tests, and exams. I have these three supplemental manuals with me today. Let's look at them together right now!

The **"I know that I need it, but..."** objection should be a lay-up for an experienced salesperson. Occasionally there may turn out to be a hidden factor that cannot be handled or solved by the sales rep. For example, the prospect may in fact want and need your product; but after a lengthy conversation with him, you discover that he lacks the authority to make the buy-decision. Which brings us to our **next** objection.

5 – "I'D LIKE TO, BUT I REALLY DON'T HAVE THE AUTHORITY..." When you get this objection, you can be pretty sure that one of two things has happened: (1) You haven't done your homework, and you've been wasting your time trying to sell the **wrong** prospect, or (2) the prospect is **lying** to you in an attempt to show you the door. So the first thing you have to do is determine whether or not the prospect is telling the truth.

If you have a hunch that you did your homework accurately and that for some reason (whatever it might be) your prospect does indeed have the authority to make the buy-decision, then you should probe further with your close. Be careful not to challenge the customer; you certainly should not be confrontational. Don't burn a bridge with someone you've just spent thirty minutes of valuable time with. In any case, you have a hunch that this person **does** have the authority to say "yes." A veteran salesperson addresses this issue in the narrative below.

> *Example:*
> "I once had a prospect tell me that he really wanted to go with my product but that as a professional courtesy he needed to 'talk it over' with a colleague. I thought that I could tell that he really wanted to say 'yes' to me right then and there. I had paid dues with him for more than a year and had really expected to get the business on this personal sales call. His body language was even very positive; yet he was telling me that he just couldn't make the decision without getting the approval of a colleague."

"I decided to close again, very directly. I said, 'Fred, you know that I've really delivered for you this past year; I've gotten you every sample product you've asked for, and promptly, too. Now, here's my question to you: If it came right down to it, you **would** have the **authority** to go with my product even if your colleague didn't agree with you on the decision; isn't that right?' My directness, coupled with the warmth and sincerity of my body language, had its effect. Fred leaned back in his chair, was silent for several seconds, and then began to smile. He liked me, **and** he liked the idea of being a person in whom real authority resided. He liked me telling him that **I knew** he was the person who could make the buy-decision. My next words asked him for the business, and he proudly gave it to me, instantly!"

Of course not every situation involving the **"I'd like to, but I really don't have the authority"** objection ends on such a positive and successful note. In many cases the prospect really does **not** have the authority to make the buy-decision. How is it that a sales rep can end up in a situation trying to close a person who lacks the authority to say yes? Generally speaking, there are two ways by which this situation can occur. The salesperson may have done shoddy homework, thus pursuing a prospect who (for whatever reason - ego, perhaps) simply never bothered to inform the sales rep of his mistake. Or, the prospect may have purposely misled the salesperson. In either case, the sales rep must now "make lemonade from lemons."

The strategy at this point should be **not** to lose the investment that you have already made in the prospect - albeit the **wrong** one! Chances are that this individual has access to, maybe even real influence with, the decision maker. If so, you should be sure to cash in on this advantage. Your prospect may be just the right person to introduce you to the decision maker, and may be able to work effectively inside the company's organization to support your sales campaign. At the very least, the prospect you have wrongly prepped can most likely provide you with valuable information about the individual who has the authority to make the buy-decision.

6 – CREDIBILITY. From at least one perspective, this objection can be viewed as a good one to receive because normally a prospect will not raise it until he has heard the sales presentation and decides that he is interested. Usually the prospective customer will say something like

- "I like what you say about this product, but I've never met you."

- "You make a strong sales presentation, but I'm not familiar with your company."

- "I'm interested in what you're selling, but actually it sounds too good to be true."

- "You know, I wish you could put what you've told me here in writing for me."

- "What you're talking about sounds pretty exciting, but I lost a lot of money on something like this one time."

- "Who else have you done business with?"

Questions like these tell you that the prospect is not wanting to say, "No." In fact, he wants to say, "Yes." He just wants to be safe; he wants to be sure that you, the product or service that you are selling, and the company that you represent are worthy of his trust. This is the point in the sales interview at which you should **volunteer** information to the prospect.

Many sales reps have informational flyers or brochures printed up for just such occasions as we are talking about here. Such handouts can go a long way towards dispelling anxiety on the part of the would-be customer. Any such document should have four main parts - (1) Who you are, (2) Who your company is, (3) Who your customers are, and (4) What your product or service is. A single brochure handout works well if the product or service you sell is constant; that is, if you sell the same thing over and over again. On the other hand, if the product or service you sell is always changing, even though you continue to represent the same company, then you might do well to develop two handouts - one that contains information about yourself, your company, and your present customers, and another that provides detailed information about the product or service that you are selling at that particular point in time.

In any case, when your prospect raises the credibility objection, that is the time to walk him through the brochure(s) we have just discussed. You may have given it to him at the beginning of your sales presentation, or you may hand it to him at this moment in the interview. In either case, **now** is the time to walk him through it. Don't just refer to it or hand it to him. Go through it with the client, **point by point.** Credibility is **not** gained by nodding your head or pointing your finger in the general direction of a sales handout!

If, after walking the client through your sales brochure(s), you sense that the credibility question still exists, then you will have to probe to discover what question(s) you have not answered or what doubt you have not satisfied. Once you are able to define the prospect's **area** (focus) of doubt - you, your company, your other customers, your product/service - then you can concentrate on satisfying the credibility question. Remember, most prospects won't be satisfied with your personal opinion or other subjective information; if possible, use documented facts and figures. Numbers and statistics are usually seen by customers as being **hard** (objective) evidence or proof.

Now, ask the prospect directly if you have satisfied the question(s) he had with regard to whatever his area of doubt or uneasiness was. Get him to confirm that you **have** satisfied the credibility objection, and then move immediately to a close.

7 - "I REALLY DON'T SEE WHY I SHOULD..." This objection is not always spoken. It is sometimes a silent objection that must be sensed by the salesperson. Often, however, it is verbalized. In either case, it has to do with the prospect **not** understanding the features and benefits of the product or service that you are presenting. The potential customer, in spite of your generously provided "guide service," has lost his way on Sales Pitch Road! What an embarrassment all the way around - for your prospect **and** for you!

Admittedly, not every prospect is a good listener. Not every potential client is focused on your sales presentation. But **you are** the guide. You are **responsible** for seeing that he stays with you - seeing that he does not get lost on the little march that you are leading. By way of analogy, a family scenario comes to mind. Imagine yourself a teenager who has been given the responsibility of taking a five-year-old brother or sister with you to a neighborhood store. You return home with the items requested by your parent but **without** your young sibling. Your best answer to your parent's anxious question is, "Gosh, I don't know; he was with me when I left the store!" The obvious question here is, "How could this happen?" The answer is equally obvious: At at least one point (perhaps at many points) on the trip to the store you weren't paying attention to your sibling, and intentionally or unintentionally he gave you the slip.

This little analogy can serve as a window - a paradigm - for us to look through and learn a powerful lesson about selling. The prospect is the salesperson's young sibling. It is your responsibility to **not get home without him!** It's not always easy to keep your prospect with you, but very often he will ask questions that should tip you off that at least some of the features and benefits that you are ticking off are not registering with your would-be customer. Comments like the following should stop you in your tracks:

- "I'm not sure I see the advantage of what you're describing there."
- "I can see how **some** companies might benefit from your service."
- "I'm wondering if it would **usually** work the way you're saying."
- "Our operation is a good bit different than the ones you're talking about."
- "We tend to be pretty cautious about changing our production methods."

All of these comments, of course, are red flags. Your prospect is telling you that the features and benefits that you are describing in relation to the product or service that you are selling **don't** match the needs which he has in mind. And it goes without saying, that if the prospect doesn't see a match between what you're selling and what he needs (or wants), then you can probably hold your breath comfortably for the brief time that will elapse before he punches the key that rings up "No Sale."

But actually the comments above indicate that the prospect is listening - paying attention - to your presentation. To be sure, he's objecting; but he's also giving you an invitation to fine tune your presentation in ways that will convince him that your product or service **does** match his needs. Your fine tuning should be specific. You should explain in detail (perhaps even with pencil and paper) exactly how particular features of your product or service match the needs of the prospect, thereby offering him tangible benefits (increased profit, lowered risk, reduced costs, etc.).

8 - "IT SEEMS PRETTY COMPLICATED" OR INERTIA. In a sense, this is not really an objection. There is no specific negative issue that is being raised. The prospect is not offering an argument against making the buy-decision. Yet, there is a hesitancy - perhaps even an unwillingness - on the part of the prospect to commit to the purchase. The dictionary describes inertia as "the indisposition to motion or change." And that is precisely what is happening here. The reason for this objection, if it can be called that, is that the prospect is being asked to go somewhere that he has never been before - to do something that he has never done before. The potential customer is unfamiliar with the particular buy-receive process which faces him; he does not understand what is to happen next, or what will be required of him; so he is inclined to hesitate - to do nothing.

An example of this situation might be the first-time investor in the stock market. The prospect wants to buy a stock for investment purposes but is unfamiliar with the process; he is uncomfortable about paying for something without receiving anything tangible in return. Up to this point in the sales presentation, the broker has focused on the advantages of buying this particular stock (perhaps several different stocks); now he must spell out the **procedure** by which the prospect actually buys the stock. The broker should put pencil to paper and list the exact sequence of steps that must now occur in order for the prospect to purchase the stock.

Many a sale is lost because the salesperson takes for granted that the prospect understands the buy-receive process through which the sale-purchase takes place. It is not an unusual thing for an inexperienced sales rep to return to his office wondering why he didn't make a sale after carrying off what appeared to be a really successful sales presentation. The wise boss will ask him if he explained to the prospect **how to make** the purchase. To use a tennis analogy, you will know that you have lost "point, game, set, and match" to the **inertia** objection when your prospect **makes** the buy-decision but does **not** make the actual purchase. No doubt the whole buy-receive process seemed just too **complicated** to the prospect.

Avoid Creating Objections

Prospects will come up with enough objections on their own to keep you challenged, frustrated, and amused; so don't do or say things that will help them create objections that they might otherwise not have thought of. Objections often arise as a direct result of too much conversation - too much presentation - rather than from any real problem with the product or service being sold. Here are some ways to avoid inviting objections:

- Always reflect a positive mental attitude in your sales presentation; any hint of pessimism or doubt on your part breeds uncertainty in your prospect.

- Speak with confidence and conviction; a wishy-washy tone creates doubt.

- Avoid presenting too much information; unnecessary information generates unnecessary questions.

- Be concise and to the point; brevity builds confidence.

- Constantly anticipate your prospect's response; guard against being surprised or caught off guard by a question or comment.

- Always use written notes for your sales presentation; "winging it" can result in your losing control of the flow of the sales interview.

Don't Answer Objections Before They're Raised

Detective story fans are familiar with the plot which, as the mystery draws to a close, has the principal suspect incriminate himself by attempting to answer questions about his activities or whereabouts before they have been asked. By saying too much too soon the suspect plunges himself into a situation which, adroitly exploited by a sharp-witted detective, all too quickly reveals the blatant guilt of the suspect. Readers of these stories smile at the irony of seeing the criminal inadvertently nail shut his own coffin.

Without meaning to draw a parallel between the crook in a paperback mystery novel and a professional salesperson, there is, nonetheless, a lesson to be learned from the little scenario just sketched. As you move through your sales presentation, your prospect will most likely raise questions from time to time - questions that to you (with your much greater in-depth knowledge of the product or service that you are selling) may seem very close to being objections. Your instant inclination (a defensive reaction) may be to **answer** them. **Don't!**

Make a mental note of the questions as they occur; even plan to answer them as objections later on if that becomes necessary. But for the moment, just answer them directly and briefly, or say that you will be dealing with them a little later in your presentation. Move forward smoothly with your pre-planned presentation, and by no means give any indication to your prospect that one of his off-the-cuff questions has hit you with the impact of a sniper's bullet. After all, if you have done your homework, no question from **any** prospect should intimidate you. Remember, all objections are opportunities - invitations to **sell**!

Answering objections before they have been formally raised may create anxiety and uncertainty in your prospect's mind. A prospect may begin to probe deeply into a particular area relating to your product/service if you plant the seed of doubt by answering prematurely an objection that he did not consciously intend to raise. The following scenario illustrates this point:

> ***Example:***
> Electronic Copier Salesperson: Mr. Jones, this copier is our very best machine - the top of our line. It can handle 25,000 copies a month and only has to be serviced, on average, after every 30,000 copies. This new model has many features that make it superior to all of our older units.
>
> Prospect: Well, now that gives me something to think about. We run about 40,000 copies a month. I guess that means we would need a service call about every three weeks. I was hoping we could get by without needing service more than about once every six weeks..... And did you say that your older models had to be serviced pretty often?

In this instance the sales rep has answered an unspoken objection relating to his copier's productivity-service ratio. In so doing, he has raised a serious question in the mind of the prospect. The rule about answering objections before they are raised directly and formally is: **Don't!**

Close After Handling Each Objection

Many salespeople think that after they have successfully handled an objection that the sale will automatically fall into their lap. Such a thing rarely happens, especially if the objection is raised at a relatively early point in the sales presentation. A smart sales rep will close each time he handles an objection. Naturally, most prospects will not make a buy-decision early in a sales interview, but by closing after each objection has been handled, the salesperson at least gets confirmation from the prospect that that **particular** obstacle to the buy-decision has been removed. The stage is then set with a positive tone for moving smoothly forward with the sales presentation.

Another point to consider here is that many prospects are well informed, at least in a general way, about the product or service that is being presented to them. In fact, the prospect may have a laundry list going into the sales interview consisting of several points he intends to ask about. The salesperson has no way of knowing how long this list is; it may have only two points, or it may have ten. Thus, the salesperson who closes after successfully handling the third objection, even though it arises early in the sales interview, may just get the buy-decision right then and there. The prospect may have had only three points on his objection list, and having had all of them answered is ready to be closed.

Handle Smoke Screens

Smoke screen excuses. Smoke screen stalls. What are they? They're not the real thing; that's what! But they're real enough to get rid of you - real enough to enable a prospect to avoid talking with you or seeing you. Whether you sell on the phone or in person (or both), you will encounter many stalls from prospects who don't want to talk with you. Of course, if you do a good job of prospecting and qualify your prospects carefully, you can minimize the number of smoke screen excuses that are blown your way. But even if you're selling a product or service that a prospect really needs, you must remember that most likely there are a lot of **other** salespeople out there selling the same product or service.

Most prospects don't want to talk to a dozen different sales reps about the same product, so they screen out salespersons by tossing out one-liners designed to chill the blood of the most fervent sales rep. These one-liners (of course they can be longer) are called smoke screens because they, like smoke, are chimerical and lack substance. They're also called smoke screens because they're used by prospects who are trying to hide from you; they provide cover for the person who wants to keep distance between himself and salespeople. The following list contains some of the most often heard stalls or smoke screens.

- "I don't have any money."
- "I'm too busy to talk right now."
- "I'm not interested."
- "I don't want to buy anything right now."
- "Not now, call me next month."
- "Sorry, but I do all my business with another salesman."
- "What are you selling?"
- "Just send me your card."
- "Where did you get my name?"
- "Thanks, but everything in that area is well taken care of."

Of course it's easy to think of short, snappy retorts to make to these blatant stalls. For example, to the prospect who says:

"What are you selling?"
    You could say, "What are you buying?"

"Send me your card."
    You could say, "What should I attach to it?"

"Where'd you get my name?"
    You could say, "It was on my desk."

But winning the duel of repartee is **not** likely to open doors very often for salespersons, though it does occasionally happen. Some prospects like to play tough to test the mettle of sales reps and respond positively to a good-humored and spontaneous retort. But far more frequently the sales rep would be well advised to respond to an obvious smoke screen with a calm, logical, straightforward response. For example, take the prospect who flippantly says, "I don't have any money." A good response might be something like the following:

> *Example:*
> "I'm not calling you about **spending** money; I'm calling you about a product that I know will be so cost-effective in your operation that it will **save** you money - a good deal of money. I know the product that you're presently using, and I've put together some comparative figures to

show you just how much I can save you on a monthly basis. All I want is an opportunity to talk business with you - facts and numbers. If you don't like what you see and hear; I'm gone. I'm awfully busy myself. When can we meet?"

This kind of response cuts right through the smoke screen and puts a straightforward, serious business proposition in the prospect's lap. If he cares about his cost of operation and profit margin, he'll turn around in a heartbeat and schedule an appointment with the sales rep. This is the way to deal with smoke screens.

Summary

This chapter is absolutely critical for the salesperson who intends to "make a career of it," bagging the tough ones as well as getting the "layups." No real skill is required to "write up" the easy ones; any salesperson with a pulse and the slightest hint of a respiratory function can get the business of the prospect who can't wait to sign on the dotted line. But the *big* fish don't usually jump into the angler's net or creel without a fight. And the "fight" is the thing! That's where handling objections comes in. If you're a sales rep who's in it for the long haul and one who has a strong distaste for hoisting white flags and taking cover just because a prospect has the audacity to fire a shot or two across your bow, then this chapter has been for *you*! It's your cup of tea because it's all about how to handle the prospect who wants to shoot it out. Remember, the prospect who shoots (objects) is *engaged*, *connected*, to your sales presentation. He's interested or he wouldn't be objecting. Always remember that the posting of an objection is an invitation for you to *handle* (dispose of) it.

This chapter is *absolutely* comprehensive in spelling out the different kinds of objections that prospects raise. If you represent a *good* product or service (one that has real value), and if you *know* your product or service, then you're just a step away the bank. Any serious salesperson can learn the objections presented in this chapter *and* the methods for handling them. It's just a matter of studying the various objections and then gaining experience in dealing with them.

After every sales call or interview you should analyze what objections were raised and how you handled them. Sometimes it's not easy to identify an objection for what it really is in the midst of a fast-moving sales interview. And, of course, if you mis-diagnose a particular objection, you may also mishandle it. Sometimes such a mistake may cost you a sale, at least for the short term. But there's always tomorrow. There will always be another day. Meanwhile you are *learning*! And your increased knowledge will give you increased power, and in no time at all you will have become a real force to be reckoned with - a skillful, experienced salesperson who *thrives* on handling the objections of prospects. You probably will even develop a mental outlook that says, "If I can just get him to object, then I *know* I can get his business!"

7

CLOSING

Introduction

WHAT IS CLOSING? Closing is what a salesperson does to get a positive decision - a "yes" - from the prospect. Closing is asking the customer for his business. To close a prospect is to get his consent - his agreement - to buy the product or service that you are selling. If you don't know how to close, or if you are an ineffective closer, this chapter is for you!

A Way of Thinking About Closing

AN ANALOGY FROM BASEBALL. Baseball fans know that every team has players who are called "relief pitchers" - pitchers who come in to "put out the fire" when the other team is threatening to score. There are different kinds of relief pitchers - "long," "middle," "short," and "closers." A "long reliever" is a pitcher who has the ability to come into a ball game early on and work for five or six innings, maybe more. A "middle reliever" is a player who is effective for a few innings; he is frequently brought into a game around the 5th or 6th inning. A "short reliever" usually comes into a game around the 7th inning. But the "closer" - what about the closer?

The closer comes into the game when all the chips are on the table. The closer comes on when the game's end is at hand and everything that has been battled for over the past three hours is at stake. The closer comes to the pitcher's mound with one out in the 8th inning. His team is ahead 3-2, but the bases are loaded and the "power" of the opposing team's lineup is coming to the plate. His job is to get two outs and end the inning and the home team's threat. Then he will come back again in the 9th and get three more outs, and the game will be over. He may throw only ten pitches; he may pitch only seven minutes. But if he does his job, he will be one of the game's heroes.

In baseball, the closer is a specialist who may be paid $2 million or more a season. He never puts in much time in any single ball game, but the minutes that he pitches are absolutely critical to the outcome of the game.

The Salesperson as Closer

SALESPERSON HAS TO DO IT ALL. Wouldn't it be great if a salesperson could walk into a sales interview, make his presentation, handle objections, and then say to the prospect, "Sit still; I'm going to get my associate who's in the hallway to come in and close you." But, as we all know, in sales it doesn't work that way. The starting pitcher is still on the mound when it comes time to close. As a salesperson, you have to throw both the opening and closing pitches.

IMPORTANCE OF CLOSING. Some salespeople think that if they make a strong and substantive sales presentation they will just naturally get the business without having to put the prospect "on the spot" by asking for it, but in the real world that rarely happens. Research consistently shows that 80% or more of all sales are made on the 5th call or close. Another 10% are made on the 4th call or close, leaving a total of only 10% that are made prior to the 4th call or close. The point here is that the successful salesperson must not only close, he must close repeatedly with the same prospect.

To return to our baseball analogy, the closer who comes into a ball game in the 8th inning knows that he will have to throw more than one pitch. In fact, he may end up throwing twenty pitches to a single hitter who keeps fouling them off. (Batters have responsibilities, too.) Batters who keep hitting foul balls are like prospects who keep raising objections. But sooner or later there will be resolution to the conflict between the pitcher and batter. One thing is certain - the pitcher will not just throw five or six pitches and walk off the field. He gets credit for a "win" or a "save" only if he finishes his job.

NO PAYOFF WITHOUT THE CLOSE. As a salesperson, you spend a great deal of time prospecting for qualified customers and preparing for sales presentations. By the time you actually sit down with a qualified prospect for an appointment, you have a considerable investment of time and energy riding on the outcome of the sales interview. You must be willing to close your prospect repeatedly during the course of your sales presentation, even in the face of rejection, or else you lose by default all that you have invested in the prospect prior to that present moment.

The point is obvious: To be successful in sales, you have to be willing to close a prospect many times in order to get a sale. If you lack the nerve or determination to close repeatedly with the same prospect during a sales interview, you will never be a successful salesperson. Abandon all false illusions and seek a different profession immediately!

GIVE YOURSELF A CHANCE. But wait! Before you give up on a career in sales, consider this: Most of today's top salespeople started out not knowing how to close a prospect and being scared to try. You can overcome your fear of closing, and you can learn how to be an expert closer.

Reasons Why Salespersons Fear Closings

Being afraid to close a prospect is perfectly natural. There is an old saying ,"Fools rush in where angels fear to tread." Most of us aren't fools, and so we are naturally hesitant to attempt something that has the potential for making us feel that we have been rejected or that we have failed. But there are a couple of other old sayings that are relevant to this discussion. Shakespeare's Hamlet said, "Readiness is all," and for many years young scouts were raised with the motto, "Be prepared." The point here is that our fear of any particular thing can be diminished, or even done away with altogether, if only we understand and prepare ourselves for dealing with the thing that we must face. So let's consider the several reasons why salespeople are frightened about the task of closing a prospect:

1 - Lack of confidence in the product or service being sold.
2 - Failure to establish meaningful rapport with the prospect.
3 - Failure to handle effectively objections raised by the client.
4 - Defeatist attitude toward making the sale.
5 - Fear of personal rejection by the prospect.

Now let's examine each one of these reasons individually.

1. LACK OF CONFIDENCE IN THE PRODUCT OR SERVICE BEING SOLD. How can a sales rep not have confidence in what he is selling. Simple! He doesn't know enough about his product or service. He lacks product information. Nobody can be confident about a product or service if they are only half informed about the features and benefits of what they are selling. Knowledge is power! Information gives confidence! The fully informed salesperson is usually eager to close; that's what the whole sales interview is about! If you are fully informed about what you are selling and still lack confidence in it, find another product to sell! One caution: Don't fool yourself about being fully informed with regard to the product or service you are selling. Before you walk away from a good product, be sure you know what you are leaving behind. Don't equate your own intellectual laziness with a poor product!

2. LACK OF MEANINGFUL RAPPORT WITH THE PROSPECT. Many sales reps think that rapport is established by talking about family, sports, hobbies - personal things. And it is. But it must also be established at another level - the professional level. Most salespeople are pretty good at talking about personal things and are able to get the prospect engaged in lively conversation about non-business topics, but they often lack the ability to make a smooth transition from "small talk" to professional conversation about business. An experienced observer can often see the negative body language of a prospect as he reacts to a salesperson's awkward move from personal to professional conversation. Thinking of yourself as a professional consultant will help you establish genuine rapport with a prospect at the business level, and you will find your fear of closing rapidly disappearing.

3. FAILURE TO HANDLE EFFECTIVELY OBJECTIONS RAISED BY THE PROSPECT. If you have done your homework concerning the product or service that you are selling, you should not have difficulty answering any objections that the prospect may raise. After all, you have a distinct advantage over him: The product or service being sold is **yours**. It belongs to you. You are the expert about it, not the prospect. An important part of preparing for a sales presentation is anticipating what objections the prospect may raise and then developing answers to them. The well-prepared salesperson actually hopes that the prospect will bring up various objections to the product or service he is selling because they will provide him with opportunities for selling. His attitude is: "I'm so glad you asked that question."

4. DEFEATIST ATTITUDE TOWARD MAKING THE SALE. The defeatist attitude or "whipped dog" mental outlook is deadly. There are two things that you can do to absolutely abolish it. The first is to know your product; the second is to know your prospect. If you have a thorough knowledge of the product or service that you are selling, and thereby great confidence in its value, you are half-way there towards beating a defeatist attitude. All that remains to be done is to qualify your prospect so that you know that he needs your product or service. If you are convinced that you have a valuable product and you are certain that your prospect needs it, then a defeatist attitude on your part becomes unthinkable. If you are unable to close him, your attitude can only be, "Too bad for him. He missed out on a really good thing."

5. FEAR OF PERSONAL REJECTION BY THE PROSPECT. Every salesperson knows that he is selling more than just a product or service; to at least some degree he is selling himself. So it is not surprising that salespeople often feel personally rejected when they fail to make a sale. But the very idea of the existence of a connection between a lost sale and personal rejection needs to be examined closely. The myth of the salesperson possessed of so much charisma that he could "sell ice to Eskimos" is precisely that - a myth. The environment in which most of today's selling is done places heavy emphasis upon the merit and price of the product or service being sold; and when a competent salesperson loses a sale of his particular product or service, he should in no way interpret that loss as personal rejection by the prospect.

Preparedness Checklist for Salesperson

In a moment now we will move on to study a number of different kinds of closes that can be used during a sales presentation, but first we will pause to evaluate how well prepared you are for the sales interview. The questions below focus on (1) the salesperson himself, (2) his knowledge of the product or service being sold, and (3) his knowledge of the prospect.

THE SALESPERSON:

1. Do you know at what points in your sales presentation you will close this prospect?
2. Are you ready to be a good listener?
3. Do you know what to do after your prospect gives you his first "no."?
4. Have you decided on the specific purpose of the call or appointment?
5. Are you prepared to ask more qualifying questions?
6. Do you have an optimistic attitude toward your interview with this prospect?

THE PRODUCT:

1. Are you prepared to tell a full story, covering all pertinent facts in a set format, taking into consideration that the prospect will interrupt you from time to time?
2. Can you explain in detail to the prospect the specific features of your product or service and the benefits they will afford him?
3. Do you know what the prospect will lose if he chooses not to buy your product or service?
4. Do you have answers for any objections that the prospect may raise about the product or service you are selling?
5. Do you have solid evidence to support all of the claims that you will make about your product or service?

THE PROSPECT:

1. Do you have at least a basic understanding of who the prospect is and what he does?
2. If he runs a business, do you have a reasonable knowledge of its operation?
3. Have you figured out how your product or service fits into the list of things that he needs, either personally or for his business?
4. Do you know how you will "break the ice" with him?

5. Does the prospect have the power and authority to make the buy-decision?

By dealing with these questions and preparing yourself so that you can answer all of them positively, you will go a long way toward dispelling any remaining fear that you might have regarding your ability or willingness to close the prospect repeatedly during the sales interview.

Types of Closes

We turn now to examine the several different closes traditionally used by salespersons. We have divided them into two groups: (1) Low Pressure and (2) High Pressure. A low pressure close is one that pushes the prospect gently and subtly. A high pressure close is one that pushes the prospect strongly and directly.

LOW PRESSURE CLOSES:

The Choice Close. This close pushes the prospect to choose something - the date of a second appointment, the size or amount of product he is interested in, his preference of color or style, etc. But it does not ask him to make the buy-decision. It is a very gentle close. In fact, it is a sort of pre-close. It requires the prospect to make a response but at the same time allows him the feeling that he is postponing to another day any real decision about buying the product or service.

> *Example:* "I know you want to think about this a little longer, so we'll talk about it again the next time we get together. I'll be in your area next week on Tuesday and Thursday. Which day is best for you?"
>
> Notice that the question is put to the prospect in a way that does not allow for him to avoid altogether the setting up of a second appointment. The question is not open-ended ("Can I see you next week?"), but rather, is stated in a way that requires the prospect to agree to another interview.

The Take Action Close. This is very similar to the close just discussed but moves the prospect slightly closer to making the buy-decision. The salesperson asks the prospect to take some particular action that will facilitate the sale. The prospect may be asked to fill out an application form, provide his social security number, spell out his full legal name, etc.

> *Example:* A salesperson has been discussing a life

insurance policy with a prospect for several minutes. The prospect appears to be undecided. The agent, hoping to move forward toward a sale, says, "Mrs. Smith, here's our application form. Why don't you just take a few minutes to fill it out, and we'll see if we can get you approved through our Life Underwriting Department."

The prospect might have been intimidated and scared off if the salesperson had used a more direct and assertive close. Imagine the agent saying, "Mrs. Smith, this is the policy for you. What do you say? We can't fill out the application form until you make a decision." Very likely the prospect would have said that she needed "to think about it some more" and left the office. But the "Take Action Close" used in our example above sets the stage for the prospect to be "approved" by the company, thus providing the salesperson with the future opportunity to tell Mrs. Smith the "good news" and close her on the policy.

The Assumptive Close.   Sometimes called the "Assertive Close," this is a strategy that works well with a prospect who is very close to saying "yes" but hasn't actually done so. It is a close to use with a prospect who has raised no serious objections and has responded positively to much of the sales presentation. It purposely avoids asking directly for the buy-decision. Instead, it moves the sales interview forward in a way that takes for granted (assumes) that the prospect has already said "yes."

> *Example:* A securities salesperson is concluding a sales interview with a prospect who is looking for a no-risk investment opportunity. The broker wraps up the session by saying, "All right, Mr. Jones, since you want safety, income, and no risk, we'll buy $5,000. worth of U.S. Treasury Bonds. Your investment will be backed by the full faith and credit of the government, and your interest will be paid to you semi-annually."

This close will almost always work smoothly if the salesperson has read the prospect correctly. When carried out to perfection, it has the great advantage of making the prospect feel that he wasn't sold anything, but rather, that the salesperson just carried out his desire.

The Something for Nothing Close.   This is a close to be used with the prospect who is standing right on the front edge of the diving board. He wants to jump but needs a tiny push. He has already made the buy-decision but needs to pacify his conscience that is telling him that he was "too easy." The unusual thing about this close is that, in many cases, the prospect will ask for it. He will want a "free delivery" or "free installation." Or he may want the dealer to pay the tax on the sale. But the point is always the same: He wants to feel that he drove a hard bargain. Generally, he will be satisfied with a very small or tokenistic concession on the part of the seller. This sales strategy is sometimes referred to as the "Tokenism Close."

> *Example:* A car salesperson has been talking with a prospect for more than an hour. It is clear that the customer is anxious to buy a very expensive utility vehicle. It is equally clear that he thinks the sticker price is a bit high and that he should, one way or another, get some sort of break from the dealership. The prospect has repeatedly mentioned how nice it would be to have a "dealer installed cellular phone." The salesperson has worked his timing just right when he finally says to the customer, "Look, you know we sell these 4-wheel vehicles just as fast as we get them in. I've got two other guys who want this one. But I'll tell you what - If we can make this deal today, I'll put that phone in there for you. No charge."

The potential problem inherent in this close is that the salesperson may offer the lagniappe too quickly, thereby diminishing its value, and consequently, its effectiveness.

The Third Party Close. This close might better be called the "I was talking with your neighbor, Fred" Close because that name really describes what it attempts to do. In order to gain credibility with the prospect, the salesperson makes reference to a third party - a neighbor, friend, or business acquaintance of the prospect with whom he is doing business. This strategy is often used as an opening "ice breaker" at the start of the sales interview but can also be used effectively as a close later on.

It is usually considered a low pressure close because a prospect who is offering strong resistance to a sales presentation is not likely to be influenced in any decisive way by being told that you are doing business with "Fred." On the other hand, a prospect who is close to saying "yes" already might very well be pushed on over the edge by the reference to one of his neighbors or friends. There is, however, a risk factor in using this close. Its effectiveness depends largely upon the prospect having a positive opinion concerning "Fred's" good judgment. Before using "Fred" as a close, you should know something about his local reputation or you could end up damaging rather than enhancing your own credibility.

> *Example:* A salesperson who sells farm supplies - chemical fertilizers, pesticides, etc. - has developed a good relationship with two farmers who live relatively close to the prospect with whom he is now talking. The prospect has made the point that the products being discussed are "pretty much the same" wherever you buy them, and he's been doing business with a local farm store for "quite a while." At this point the sales rep says, "Well, you're right about that; the products are about the same, but my company thinks that service makes a difference. We deliver what we sell, and usually on the same day we get the order. A couple of your neighbors, Bill Tuttle and Ralph Dalton, have been very happy with our service. Maybe you should give us a try."

> *Example:* Oskar and Xanthia Bartok mailed back a response card to the Ear Buster Home Alarm Company. A sales rep set up an appointment with them and a few days later is talking with them in their home. Knowing that they have a real interest in his product, the salesperson uses the "Third Party Close" as an opener: "I know that you folks have read our flyer that we sent out in the mail, so you already know a good bit about our system. Maybe a good place to start would be just to tell you who some of our very satisfied customers are."

> The sales rep is using the "Third Party Close" as a warm and friendly confidence-building strategy. He should be able to establish strong credibility quickly and close the Bartoks in just a few minutes.

While the "Third Person Close" is most often used as a low pressure close, there are certain high pressure sales situations in which it also can be used effectively. So we will discuss it again in the next section.

High Pressure Closes:

The Directive Close. This close does what its name implies. It directs the prospect to take a certain action. The salesperson tells the prospect exactly what to do. It can be effectively used toward the end of a lengthy sales interview if the prospect has been convinced of the merit of the product or service being sold. On the other hand, if he has raised objections that were not satisfactorily answered, he may be offended and put off by this type close.

> *Example:* A sales rep for a frozen food home service plan has explained at rather great length the many advantages afforded by the plan. The prospect has listened with interest and asked a few questions during the sales presentation. The salesperson, sensing no serious reservations on the part of the prospect, says, "Mrs. Logan, You simply must try the plan for at least six months. You'll see for yourself that it's everything I've said, and more."

The Ask for It Close. Very similar to the "Directive Close," this strategy differs from it by asking rather than telling. The salesperson summarizes the reasons why the prospect should buy his product or service and then asks directly for the buy-decision. The prospect is thus placed in the position of feeling obligated to refute the reasons for buying just given, or else agree to the purchase.

> *Example:* An individual who sells telecommunication devices and who has just demonstrated two very similar fax machines to a prospect who seems impressed but somewhat concerned about price says, "There's really not that much difference between these two units; you can save sixty dollars by buying this Executive Assistant model. How about letting me write it up for you?"

The Urgency Close. This is a strategy that seeks to persuade the prospect that the product or service being offered is scarce and/or available at reduced price only for a very limited time. Lines like, "The sale ends today" and "There are only a few left" come to mind. And it is often couched in an "if" clause. For example: "If I can still get it for you at that price (or in that color, etc.). It is a very high pressure tactic that can be used effectively if the salesperson convinces the prospect of two things: (1) that the scarcity or urgency is real, and (2) that the gain to be netted by acting immediately is significant.

> *Example:* A stock broker tells a client that Acme, Inc. is trading at $15 per share. He goes on to explain that on Friday the company will release its quarterly earnings report which will show a big increase in sales and earnings. He then attempts to close the client by saying, "Mr. Wilson, the numbers that are due out on Friday could

influence the stock dramatically. It is already up a quarter of a point today. Probably the market has caught wind of what's happening and is starting to buy it. If you want to have the best possible chance of making money on this deal, I think we should buy right now!"

The Summary Close. This close is not always a high pressure close. In fact, many salespersons use it routinely for easy and tough sales alike. But it is often used in situations where the prospect is still not persuaded to buy at the conclusion of the sales presentation. What it does is summarize all of the reasons - the positives - for buying the product or service being offered.

> *Example:* A salesperson who does direct sales of personal care and household products has completed her sales presentation to a middle-aged couple. They have asked a good many questions during the half-hour session and appear to be undecided as to whether they want to switch from the brand of products they are presently using.

> The sales rep attempts to close them by saying, "I know it's not easy to think of switching loyalties after using one brand of products for a long time, but there are several reasons why you might want to go ahead and make the move to the Sunflower line. Our products are chemically engineered to be environmentally friendly; they are competitively priced and fully guaranteed. We offer a wider variety of products than any of our competitors, and we have a customer rebate plan that saves money for repeat customers. You won't be sorry that you made the move."

> *Example:* A securities salesperson concludes her sales presentation by saying, "Mr. Fernsmith, this tax-free bond offers you income on a monthly basis that is federally and state tax-exempt. The current yield will be 7.5% tax-free. Your principal and interest are guaranteed and insured with regard to the timely payment of both interest and principal. I believe this investment is exactly what you've been looking for."

The Analytic Close. You could call this strategy the "Balance Sheet Close" because it is used when a prospect wants to see all of the "debits and credits" - all of the pro's and con's - relating to the product or service being offered. This prospect will not make the buy-decision until he has balanced the risks versus the potential gains involved in the purchase which is being recommended. There is no point in trying to sidestep his desire to analyze the many factors involved. He will not buy if he is denied what he considers to be an objective analysis of the facts. The salesperson who knows his product and believes in it will not be anxious about using this close. In fact, if you can handle this closing strategy skillfully, you should make a sale every time you use it.

Since the prospect is "looking for trouble," so to speak - looking for ways in which he might become vulnerable if he makes the purchase, the best thing to do is lay out for him up front the various risks that are inherent in the deal. The risks should not be treated lightly. Neither should they be exaggerated, but you will lose credibility if you attempt to understate them. This prospect will warm to your forthrightness in describing them. The rest is easy. You simply list all of the positives - all of the potential gains and rewards - that may accrue to the prospect if he decides to buy. If the pluses don't outweigh the negatives, either you haven't done your homework, or you're selling the wrong product.

> ***Example:*** A real estate agent has been talking with a client for several weeks about a particular property. The property is a rather unusual one, and several things about it could be considered as strong reasons for not buying it. But there are also factors that could make its purchase a very profitable investment. The agent and the prospect are meeting once again to discuss the property.
>
> The salesperson says, "You know, as you've pointed out, there are several things about this property that kind of jump out at you like red flags, but there are a lot of pluses, too. Why don't we just make a list of the pro's and con's about this place. Let's look at the negatives first. It's an old house and needs a fair amount of work. On one side of it there's a pretty ordinary neighborhood made up of modest homes. On another side is about forty acres of undeveloped land. And, of course, we know that the house will be tied up in an estate for another couple of months or so. I know that a lot of buyers wouldn't want to fool with it."
>
> "But let's look at the other side of the picture. Although the house is old, it's structurally sound and has almost 3000 square feet under roof. For a reasonable cost it can

be turned into a real mansion. The neighborhood on the east side is pretty modest; I grant you that. But it's stable and most likely will continue to be. The undeveloped forty acres on the west side of the property, from all present indications, is almost certain to be turned into a city park and golf course. It also appears that a new shopping center will be built on the other side of the park. Finally, even though the property is presently tied up in an estate, the executor has the authority to sign a binding sales contract with you. By making a commitment now, you can save thousands of dollars, which is not to mention the fact that the property will no doubt double in value as soon as the city begins work on the park and golf course. I feel strongly that the buyer of this property will really come out ahead."

The analytical close can be handled in a number of different ways. Often a single negative will be presented, discussed, and balanced against the corresponding positive. Sometimes (as above) the negatives will be presented and discussed as a group, to be followed by the presentation and discussion of the positives. It is very important to allow the prospect to have input during this close. His input will enable you to focus on precisely those factors that are holding him back. The example above, for the sake of brevity, does not exhibit the dialog that would normally take place between salesperson and prospect.

The Talk Dollars Close. This close is for the prospect who has a single focus - money. He wants to know how the product or service you are selling will make or save him money. The thing to be done here is to list and explain the specific ways that you can make (or save) money for the prospect. It is very important not to forget that many products and services produce indirect financial benefits, earnings and/or savings. For example, suppose you are selling a training program for employees. Some corporate managers see training programs only as a cost. But in reality, such programs often effect significant savings and/or profits for a company by reducing employee turnover and increasing employee productivity.

Example: A carpet salesperson in a large department store has been talking with a customer for nearly an hour. The individual has settled on a carpet which he really likes, but he feels that it is too expensive. He tells the clerk that he can buy a similar carpet at a discount outlet for about 30% less.

The salesperson listens courteously and then responds, "I

think you're right; you probably can save money on the initial cost by buying at an outlet, but there are a couple of things that you need to consider. There is no manufacturer's warranty on carpet sold at discount stores. I know you don't care about a warranty, per se, but buying carpet without one could end up costing you a lot of money if you have to replace it in a year or two. The other thing is that we install the carpet we sell at a fraction of the cost that you would have to pay an independent contractor. These two factors are why I think you will come out real money ahead by buying from us."

The Third Party Close. We discussed this close in the first section dealing with "Low Pressure Closes," but it is also used as a more intense close in certain situations. Telemarketers who call prospects from half-way across the country usually try to sell their product or service on the basis of their claim that it is the "best bargain," the "finest quality," or the "best opportunity;" but often they meet with strong resistance because the prospect perceives them as just another unfamiliar voice calling from an unknown place. So, when their high-pressure pitch based on the product's own (or potential) merit falls flat, they often make one final effort to establish credibility with the prospect and close the sale by using the "Third Party Close."

> *Example:* A telemarketer for a large, retail department store chain is selling extended warranties for major home appliances (air conditioners, washers, dryers, ranges, refrigerators, etc.). She has been talking for several minutes to a homeowner who has taken the position that major appliances that don't break down during the first six months after purchase, probably will not break down at all, at least not for many years. The salesperson's arguments to the contrary have been rebuffed.
>
> The telemarketer makes one last effort to close the prospect by saying, "I know you have some real reservations about the value of extended warranties, and I realize that I'm a kind of faceless nobody on the other end of the phone line here, but let me at least tell you that several other folks in your town feel that these warranties are a good investment and have purchased them. I've asked them for permission to use their names, and I'll be glad to tell you who they are if you'd like to know. It's just

possible that some of them may be your neighbors."

In situations of this kind the "Third Party Close" is a sort of last-ditch stand that may not succeed, but there is no downside in using it since the sale appears to be lost. There is always a chance that a local third party "endorsement" may give you credibility and turn the prospect around.

The "I almost forgot" Close. This is a close of dubious value and anemic integrity, but many salespersons use it when everything else has failed. The situation in which it is used looks like this:

> *Example:* The sales rep has put forward his best arguments for the value of the product or service that he is selling. He has gone over features and benefits right down to the last one that is worth mentioning. The net result for all his effort is a big fat zero. So, he decides to punt.
>
> He leans back and shifts gears, moving the conversation away from the sales presentation to personal and social banter. The prospect also leans back and seems to relax and drop his barriers to the sales pitch. After a few minutes of this interlude, the salesperson suddenly and with great flare says, "Oh, I just remembered..... I can't believe that I forgot to tell you about one of the most important features of my product. Oh no......" If the rep is lucky, the prospect will show at least an inkling of curiosity about what precious piece of the sales pitch was forgotten, and the salesperson will eagerly oblige by describing with great gusto the vastly significant, but "forgotten," feature of his product, concluding his spiel with one final close.

This is a very risky close to attempt using. In the first place, it is highly unlikely that a sales rep would forget to mention the most important feature of the product he is selling. In the second place, unless the salesperson is a consummate actor, the whole performance (for that is what it is) will come off as phony and the net gain for the rep will most likely turn out to be a total loss. Nonetheless, it can work; and salespersons of the "Never say die" ilk use it without a moment's hesitation (which, of course, is the only way that it can ever be used effectively).

How to Close: Do's and Don'ts

Do Control Your Frame of Mind.

1. Have a positive mental attitude. Nothing affects your sales success more than your own mental outlook. There may be things about yourself and your situation in life that you can't change (at least in the short term), but your attitude is entirely up to you. Developing a positive mental attitude - PMA - will give you an edge over everyone else.

2. Surround yourself with other PMA's. Sustaining a positive mental attitude is much easier when you surround yourself with other people who are upbeat and enthusiastic. Attitudes are infectious. By surrounding yourself with people who refuse to get discouraged, you will find the support that you need for the tough period between sales successes. Conversely, avoid negative salespeople like the plague. You don't need an associate putting doubts in your mind or dragging you down with cynical, hopeless predictions.

3. Think of yourself as a winner. Focus on the successful closes you have already made. You have a record of accomplishment to build on. You will only get better with experience. Take your winning attitude with you on every sales call. You will develop the habit of expecting success, and that expectation will become a self-fulfilling prophecy.

4. Close with confidence and conviction. Always ask for a sale with confidence. Your manner should say to the prospect, "Everyone says 'yes' to me." He should perceive that you will be surprised if he says "no." Don't be arrogant, just strong and confident. After all, you've done your homework; you believe in what you're selling. Why shouldn't you be confident?

Do Sell Your Product or Service.

1. Create pride in your product or service. When you close a prospect, show him why he can be proud to own whatever it is that you are selling. Make him want to own it. Set the table for his thinking that those who don't have what he is buying are not as fortunate as he.

2. Use repetition; be persistent. Don't be hesitant to repeat strong parts of your sales presentation. Make further explanations, and repeat closes that you have already used. It is not unusual for an experienced salesperson to make ten or more closes in a single sales interview. Of course you could pack up and leave after your first close is rejected, but that doesn't mean that the prospect doesn't need your product or service. It only means that you gave up and quit. The more times you sell and close a prospect, the more you will demonstrate how strongly you believe in the product you are selling. Your personal product-confidence should generate credibility for you with the prospect.

If, after all your efforts, a prospect appears unmovable, make an appointment for another day. Communicate to him that you believe strongly in your product or service and that you intend to persuade him to your point of view regardless of how long it takes. Most prospects will be impressed by your determination.

3. Motivate the undecided buyer. Sometimes a prospect seems to be in a buying mood but does not respond to any of your closes. When this happens, you should back up and determine if he is being held up by any of the following questions:

- Should I buy now or later?
- Is this a good deal?
- Am I doing the right thing?
- Can I lose money?
- Should I stick with what I already have?
- Is it worth the price?
- Should I consult other professional people?
- Have I given this enough thought?
- Can I make or save money?

If it turns out that he is concerned about one or more of these questions, then you must help him answer them in ways that will motivate him to make the buy-decision. At this point, knowing as much as you now do about the prospect, ask yourself, "What would be the very best close for me to use with this person?" Then use it, keeping in mind that most people are motivated by one (or more) of the following four things: (1) need, (2) greed, (3) thrift, and (4) status.

4. Handle objections after a close, and close again. When you present a close and the prospect responds with an objection, you should pause long enough to be sure you understand it. Then you should tell the prospect that you agree with his concern(s) and that you see his perspective, but that you have an answer to his objection. In most cases, if you acknowledge a prospect's fear, address it, and counterbalance it with facts, you will be able to disarm the objection and move on to a strong close.

5. Use forceful, direct words. The words that you use to lead into your close should be strong and purposeful, not timid or indirect. They should be carefully planned before you make a sales presentation. Listed below are some pattern sentences that can be modified and personalized for use in many different closes.

- There's no question about it; this is the right time to make this investment.
- You have an opportunity here to get a great price on this product.
- I'm telling you straight; I want to build a long-term relationship with you.
- It turns out that this product is even better than I thought it was.
- Plain and simple; you're going to make money on this investment.
- This product/service is too good to pass by.
- Do you realize the potential of this product/service?
- Here are the numbers. What do you think?
- This is a tremendous opportunity, period.
- The potential for profit far outweighs the risk factors.
- I've done my homework; I have no reservations about this product.
- Look at how much money you will save.
- Here's a list of the benefits you will gain.
- These are the facts.
- There aren't many left.
- The window of opportunity is about to close.
- I understand your needs; this product/service will satisfy them.
- Your cash-flow will be very good.
- Your expenses will be reduced.
- This product/service will give you protection.
- This service will save you time.

6. **Sell service.** One of the best closes for any sale is service - your service. When you close a prospect, don't forget to remind him of the value of the ongoing service which you will provide him. The salesperson who delivers valuable service after closing a sale not only keeps the business he has already won, but opens the door to new sales as well. Sometime within the first month after you have made a sale you should contact the customer and

- Ask if everything is O.K.
- Discuss any problems.
- Ask if there is anything you can do to enhance his satisfaction.
- Tell him that you intend to continue monitoring his situation.

Surveys consistently show that about 70% of the customers who stop buying from their regular suppliers do so because they are dissatisfied with the service they have received.

DO USE FINESSE.

1. **Write out closes before sales interviews.** Before having a sales

interview, whether on the phone or in person, you should write out your entire sales presentation and all of the closes that you anticipate using. You should also anticipate the objections you are likely to receive, and write out the response and close that you will use for each one. Writing out closes in advance of a sales presentation gives you confidence. You will not recite them from memory, but you will have the confidence that comes from being "rehearsed."

2. Acknowledge prospect's freedom to choose. Communicate to the prospect that you realize that he is in a position to choose where (and from whom) he will buy the product or service you are selling; this will make him feel important. Then give him reasons why it is in his own best interest to do business with you.

3. Be casual about money. It is just about impossible to close a prospect without talking about money. He will want to know how much the product or service you are selling is going to cost. There is one rule you should always follow in this situation: Be calm and casual when talking about the price or cost of your product/service. If you become hesitant, tense, or apologetic when you begin talking about money, you are likely to trigger a negative response in the prospect. He may assume that you think the product is overpriced, or he may wonder if there are hidden costs that you are not mentioning. Stay cool and your prospect is likely to follow suit.

4. Ask for a bigger sale than you think you can get. A mistake that many inexperienced salespersons make is to aim too low when they close a prospect. You can always drop down if you propose a purchase that costs more than the prospect is willing (or able) to pay, but it is extremely difficult to take a prospect up higher after you have low-balled him. A good rule of thumb is to make an educated guess as to how big a ticket you think the prospect will go for, and then add about 25% to that number when you make your first close.

5. Recapture the prospect's attention. Sometimes you will lose a prospect's attention just as you are about to make a close. It may be that he is preoccupied with other matters or that he senses the approaching close and is attempting to escape the pressure of the sales interview. In either case you must regain his attention. One way to do this is to lower the volume of your voice dramatically, maybe by as much as 50%. Move back in your chair at the same time, thus signalling with both your voice and your body that you are withdrawing from the prospect. He will almost automatically respond by moving forward in his chair and straining to hear what you are saying. There is something about this strategy that comes close to demanding an apology from the prospect for his interruption of the communication process.

DONT'S:

1. **Don't be overanxious to close.** The skillful salesperson is careful not to let a prospect interpret his high energy-level and enthusiasm as anxiety about closing. A prospect who perceives you as being overeager to close may see you as an adversary to dismiss, rather than as a consultant to engage in conversation. Avoid giving him this kind of control and leverage. Relax and remember that you have something that he needs. You are in a position to provide him with solutions to some of his problems. There is no need for you to come across as a commission-hungry or (worse yet) desperate salesperson.

2. **Don't cut the price to get a sale.** Of course there are exceptions to this rule, but as a general practice it is a mistake to close a sale by "giving away the company store." As a salesperson, you want to add value to the product or service that you are selling, not subtract it. Reducing the price of your product or service undercuts the claims you have made regarding its quality and value. Instead of cutting prices, sell yourself and your company and the value of the service that you will provide to the customer after the sale.

3. **Don't ramble at time of close.** Inexperienced salespersons often reveal their nervousness by rambling on about nothing when it comes time to close the prospect. If you have made a solid sales presentation and answered any objections raised by the prospect, you should have no hesitation about asking for the business. Do just that, and then be silent. Nobody wants to hear a bunch of idle chatter while they are trying to make an important decision. Do not be put off if the prospect is silent for what seems like a long time after you state your close. He is thinking. Prospects who are not serious about buying will usually respond instantly to a close - negatively! Remember the old saying, "Silence is Golden"? For the skillful salesperson, that often turns out to be literally true.

Who to Close

TRY TO CLOSE ALL PROSPECTS. It's probably fair to say that a salesperson never gets the business of a prospect he doesn't close. That being the case, what's in it for the salesperson not to at least attempt to close every prospect he talks with? Sometimes experience can get in the way of a successful close. Here's the point. An experienced sales rep may conclude on the basis of a sales interview that a particular prospect is, after all, absolutely a non-prospect. In which case, the rep doesn't even bother to close the individual. Big mistake! Never walk away from a prospect without closing him. What's to lose! Never pick and choose which prospects to close and which ones to pass by. Always attempt to work and close every prospect with the same level of energy and enthusiasm.

There's an old saying which declares, "Old salesmen know everything and do nothing; new salesmen know nothing and do everything." It's always a great joy to see a new salesperson naively tackle an old prospect whom everybody knew was impossible and get the sale! The new salesperson accomplished it because he didn't know it couldn't be done! The rule here is really quite simple: Always close everybody.

When to Close

1. ASK THE PROSPECT HOW HE FEELS ABOUT THE PRODUCT. Prior to asking for a sale, you should be clear in your own mind as to how the prospect will respond. If you aren't sure, don't close. Instead, back up and evaluate the sales presentation you have made up to that point. If there are issues of interest to the prospect that need to be covered again, go back to them and present more facts and figures, more explanation. Then, if you're still uncertain as to how the prospect feels about your product/service, ask him! If he responds positively, agree with him and close the sale. If he responds negatively, listen to his objections carefully, overcome them with positive explanations, and close him.

2. CLOSE WHEN YOU FEEL LIKE IT. As you gain experience, you will almost intuitively know when a prospect is ready to close. So, when you feel the urge to close, do it! Most salespersons err in the direction of not closing soon enough or often enough. There is a natural tendency to be overly hesitant about closing, so most salespeople don't have to worry about closing a prospect too soon. On the other hand, there is a danger in not closing soon enough. A hot prospect may decide to close himself before you get around to it - just up and gives you the business (but in the amount that **he** suggests). In such a situation there is every likelihood that he will close himself "way too low." The prospect who closes himself almost always has a lot more money to spend than he gives you on a self-close. So the rule here is: If you sense that it's time to close, do it.

Reasons Why People Buy

We can better understand the dynamics of closing if we are aware of the reasons why individuals decide to buy something. Of course there are countless reasons why people buy various products and services, but the myriad causes tend to align themselves under four headings:

- Personal
- Financial
- Practical
- Social

Listed below you will find a number of phrases (just a sampling) that complete the statement, "People buy products and services in order to ...."

- make money
- save time
- reduce risk
- protect property and possessions
- avoid worry
- make things convenient
- have pleasure
- save money
- gain personal satisfaction
- enhance their image
- improve their status
- improve their personal or business relations
- satisfy their competitive urge
- reduce their taxes
- save energy
- save space
- please the seller
- fulfill a need

Studying this list from time to time should help you better understand your prospects and customers.

Summary

This has been a long and somewhat complicated chapter, probably one that you will want to read several times. No doubt it is the single most important chapter in this book because *closing* is how you *get* the business. But although there is much detailed content in this chapter, it all breaks down, really, into just three categories: (1) Having the *will* to close, (2) Having the necessary *knowledge* for closing, and (3) Having the *techniques* needed to carry out a variety of closes. As you have discovered, all three of these categories are explained in much detail.

Just to reinforce what you already know by now:

(1) Having the *will* to close has to do with overcoming any fear that you may have with regard to asking a prospect for his business, replacing that fear with a positive and confident mental attitude that gives rise to a strong desire to close a prospect as many times as it takes to make a sale.

(2) Having the necessary *knowledge* for closing a prospect has to do with

becoming an expert on the product or service that you represent and knowing how its features will answer the needs of the prospect.

(3) Having the *techniques* needed to carry out a variety of closes has to do with understanding and being able to use effectively the many high and low pressure closes explained in this chapter.

Remember, closing is both a science and an art. The science part is your knowledge of the features and benefits of the product or service that you sell. The art part is the finesse and skill with which you manage and manipulate the prospect to do your bidding.

8

CONFIRMING

Confirming a sale is getting it paid for. Confirmation of a sale is the procedure by which the salesperson moves the customer through whatever steps are required for finalizing the purchase he has agreed to. Oftentimes this is a very delicate and sensitive process; sometimes it extends over a period of time - days, weeks, even months. Experienced salespersons know that there is nothing automatic about the confirmation of a sale.

Before the Money's in the Bank

"MANY A SLIP 'TWIXT THE CUP AND THE LIP." This is an old saying that reminds us that things that seem absolutely certain sometimes turn out to be not certain at all. There are other one-liners that underscore this unsettling and somewhat cynical perspective on life:

- "Don't count your chickens until they've hatched."
- "It ain't over 'till it's over." (Yogi Berra)
- "I hope he/she doesn't leave you standing at the altar."
- "Be careful not to brag too soon."
- "Nothing's certain except death and taxes."
- "It's not over 'til the fat lady sings."

YOU MADE THE SALE. "Got it!" These are the happiest, most celebratory words a salesperson ever says. Getting a "yes" from a prospect is sometimes the result of an intense sales campaign that may have extended over several months. In the last chapter we talked about closing the prospect and getting the sale. Most salespersons would no doubt say that getting the prospect to make the buy-decision is the single most important, and usually the hardest, part of the entire sales process. But there remains one last critical element in the sales cycle.

Confirming the Sale

GETTING THE MONEY. How you do it depends on what you sell. There is a vast variety of products and services being sold in the marketplace today. Products range from the tangible (a rocking chair) to the intangible (an insurance policy). Services range from the simple (a maintenance contract on a dishwasher) to the complex (a multi-level training program for a corporation with 6,000 employees).

If you sell a rocking chair to a customer at a department store, confirming the sale is a pretty straightforward matter because payment is made right then and there at the time (and place) of the purchase. The customer may pay cash. He may charge it to his department store account or to a bank card. He may put it on layaway. But in any case, the method and terms of payment are finalized immediately upon the customer's decision to buy. There is no interval of time that elapses between the selling of the rocking chair and its being paid for. This means, of course, that the customer will not be influenced by other persons or by his own second thoughts to change his mind about buying the rocking chair. As soon as he says "yes" to the salesperson, the method of payment is confirmed, and the sales transaction is completed.

Unfortunately, many salespersons are not able to confirm their sales immediately, or even for several days after the prospect has said "yes." Sometimes a sale appears to have been confirmed but then aborts to the detriment of the salesperson and his company. The two examples below demonstrate how uncertain surefire sales sometimes turn out to be.

> *Example:* A college textbook sales rep, Robert, sold his company's physical science text to Professor Cole at a large state university in April. The order for 500 copies for September classes was signed by Professor Cole and the department head and sent to the university's bookstore. The bookstore would not order the books from the publisher until August. In May another college textbook sales rep, Mary, called on Professor Cole and persuaded her that the physical science book published by her company was superior to the one that had already been ordered. The professor said: "Too bad my order has already gone to the bookstore." To which Mary replied: "No problem; they won't be sending it to the publisher until August. There's plenty of time for you to cancel the order and put in a new one for my book." Which is exactly what Professor Cole did.

Example: A stock broker in a Florida city sold a tire dealer 12,000 shares of a particular stock for $125,000. The client paid for the stock with a personal check and later the same day called the broker to say that he needed his stock certificate right away so that he could use it as collateral to buy a warehouse of tires. The broker called his company's New York office and asked them to send the stock certificate by overnight mail. The next day the tire dealer received his certificate and bought the warehouse of tires. The broker's company, meanwhile, discovered that the customer had placed a "Stop Payment" on the $125,000 check. Two years later the brokerage firm had still not received payment for the stock.

These two examples clearly show how fragile and uncertain a closed sale can be. The case of Professor Cole illustrates how a prospect can make the buy-decision in good faith with every intention of following through on it, only to later renege on the decision due to the influence of another salesperson. The tire dealer, on the other hand, apparently never intended to pay for his stock purchase. The old saying, "Hindsight is always 20-20" seems to apply to both of these cases. If textbook salesperson, Robert, had stayed in touch with Professor Cole, he might have been able to make his sale stick. And if the Florida stockbroker's company had taken the tire dealer's check to the local bank on which it was drawn, they would never have issued the stock certificate to the conniving customer.

Because there are so many different kinds of sales, and because so many of them are so much more difficult to confirm (finalize) than the sale of the rocking chair in the department store, most salespersons need to carry out a checklist of actions after they have closed a prospect.

Things To Do After Making a Sale

Every salesperson should complete the following tasks after making a sale.

1. Congratulate the customer.
2. Outline the things that remain to be done before the sale is finalized.
3. Discuss the timetable by which they will be accomplished.
4. Ask the customer if he has any questions.
5. Terminate the sales interview.
6. Contact the customer within 48 hours to confirm completion of his responsibilities.
7. Contact the customer after one week to confirm that the sale has been

finalized.
   8. Write the customer a note thanking him for his business.

Now let's look at each one of these actions in more detail.

1. CONGRATULATE THE CUSTOMER. The very first thing to do after a customer says "yes" is to respond by saying something to him that validates and "puts on the record" the fact that he has made the buy-decision. Depending on the amount of rapport you have established with the prospect, you might accompany your words of congratulation with a handshake. There is nothing hokey about an act that is given dignity by the sincerity with which it is done.

> *Example:* A life insurance salesperson has just sold a $250,000 policy to a professional woman in her mid-thirties. The agent has had two previous appointments with the prospect in recent weeks and has established a good business relationship with her. The prospect has just said, "Yes, that's what I want to do - the $250,000 policy you've just described." The salesperson promptly stands up, extending her hand, and says, "Good, Martha! Excellent decision! This policy is very flexible and will give you a really substantial foundation that you can build on in the future."

> The salesperson does a good job here. She **congratulates** and praises the prospect, expresses enthusiasm and warmth, underscores the value of the purchase she has just made, and even opens the door to a future sale.

2. OUTLINE THE THINGS THAT REMAIN TO BE DONE BEFORE THE SALE IS FINALIZED. Often a sale cannot be consummated until a prospect accomplishes one or more additional thing(s) after he has said "yes" to the salesperson. For example, insurance companies require physical examinations for many policies. Financing has to be arranged and approved for many high dollar purchases (autos, boats, real estate, etc.). Legal documents must sometimes be prepared and signed by the prospect and other parties involved in the sale/purchase of certain products and services. In many instances, the list of additional things to be done by the prospect is very short and does not require much time. But in some situations the list can be lengthy, can involve several other persons, and can require a fair amount of time to complete. In these type situations the element of risk is magnified, and the salesperson must stay close to the prospect to ensure that nothing goes awry.

Example: A real estate agent has just closed a prospect for the purchase of a rural property - a house, a barn, two outbuildings, and 70 acres of land. But the deal itself is far from closed. After talking for several minutes with the customer about the things that remain to be done before the purchase can be finalized, the salesperson summarizes the situation for the prospect. "My office will take care of the official closing on the sale of the property, but there are several things that you must do: (1) You must arrange to have the survey done by the firm you mentioned and have them send a certified copy to my office. (2) You will need to arrange with your bank for the $120,000 mortgage loan that you will use for closing. The bank must send my office an official letter indicating its approval of the loan. (3) Since you are obtaining your own insurance on the property, you will need to bring proof of insurance to the closing. (4) You will need a certified or cashier's check in the amount of $27,500 as your down payment at the time of closing. (5) And finally, your spouse will need to be present for the closing to sign the official documents."

"I know that sounds like a lot to do, but you'll be surprised at how quickly you're able to tick these things off. And remember that I'm available at any time if you have a question, or if a problem comes up. Just give me a call. In any case, I'll be checking with you in a few days to see how things are shaping up."

3. DISCUSS THE TIMETABLE BY WHICH THEY WILL BE ACCOMPLISHED. When there are things that remain to be done before a sale can be finalized, it is the responsibility of the salesperson not only to tell the prospect what additional things he must do, but by what date(s) they must be done. This is a very straightforward procedure. The prospect has already said that he wants the product or service. At this point the salesperson is simply helping him accomplish his goal by telling him precisely when certain things need to be accomplished.

Example: In the example above (#2) the real estate agent would work with the customer to set a target date for closing, and then based on that would tell the prospect something like this: "If you want to close on September 27th, my office will need to have the survey, the bank's letter confirming the mortgage loan, and your proof of insurance certificate by Monday, the 23rd. That will give us time to draw up all the necessary documents for closing on Friday, the 27th. We won't need the down payment check until the actual closing at four o'clock on the 27th. And don't forget that your spouse will need to be present for the closing also."

4. ASK THE CUSTOMER IF HE HAS ANY QUESTIONS. This is a very important step in the confirmation process. You have given the customer a list of things to do and a timetable by which to accomplish them. Hopefully, he has not been a passive listener during your discussion of this information, but rather, has engaged in a dialogue with you about various points. In any case, it is very important that you ask him directly if he has any questions relating to either the tasks that remain to be done or the dates by which they need to be completed. And of course, if he has any questions, they should be answered to the point that he is absolutely clear about (and satisfied with) his responsibilities.

5. TERMINATE THE SALES INTERVIEW. Once the customer is clear about what happens next in terms of confirming (finalizing) the sale, you should close the sales interview promptly. Your business has been transacted. You have made the sale and informed the customer of his remaining responsibilities. Inexperienced salespersons sometimes lose sales that they have just made because they continue talking after they should have closed the interview. It is easy to say something that leads the prospect to ask a question that may cause you to have to make the sale all over again, or worse, lose it! So when you're done, "Get the hell out of Dodge," or if you're on the phone, hang up! Your final words to the new customer, however, should be to the effect that you'll be checking back with him soon with regard to the timetable discussed in #3 above.

6. CONTACT THE CUSTOMER WITHIN 48 HOURS TO CONFIRM THE COMPLETION OF HIS RESPONSIBILITIES. The "48 hours" mentioned here is really an arbitrary figure. How quickly you should check back with your customer depends in large measure upon the timetable you've set up with him (see #3 above). You don't want to annoy your client by treating him like a child, but you do want to be sure that he moves through the timetable smoothly, checking off his remaining tasks so that the sale can be finalized. Also, you want to be aware of any unforeseen obstacles that may have arisen for him so that you can help troubleshoot them. The rule here is: Don't call too soon or too often, but don't wait too long.

7. CONTACT THE CUSTOMER AFTER ONE WEEK TO CONFIRM THAT THE SALE HAS BEEN FINALIZED. Once again, the time period mentioned here, "one week," is really an arbitrary figure. You may be dealing with a situation whose timetable requires three weeks for final closure, or you may know that a particular sale will be confirmed within three days after you made the sale. In fact, in some situations you will be personally present at a meeting with the customer when the sale is finalized. The point to be mindful of is this: If you don't know for a fact that a sale has been finalized within the anticipated time frame, call the customer to find out. Never take for granted that a sale will be confirmed according to the schedule you worked out with the prospect. The most valuable time you will ever spend as a salesperson is the time you spend making sure that a sale you have already made is actually finalized. The pilot of a light plane doesn't cut the throttle when he gets to 15,000 feet just because he sees the top of the mountain. Successful salespersons never quit until a sale is finalized.

8. WRITE THE CUSTOMER A NOTE THANKING HIM FOR HIS BUSINESS. Once a sale is confirmed, don't just walk away from it as if it were finished business. In sales, business is never finished. A satisfied customer is always a qualified prospect for another sale. So, it is absolutely critical that you write a personal note to the new customer whose purchase has just been finalized. Thank him for his business and remind him that you stand ready to assist him at any time if problems should develop with regard to the product or service that you sold him. Tell him, too, that you will be in touch with him from time to time to discuss the possibility of his need for expanded use of the products or services that you sell. You should maintain a suspense file of customers who should be re-prospected at regular intervals.

Trouble-Shooting Problem Cases

WHEN SOMETHING GOES WRONG. Up to this point, we've dealt with the procedure of confirming a sale after the prospect has said "Yes." We've seen that the process can be complicated and extend over a period of time, but we have focused on the type of sale that gets finalized in a fairly routine manner. We turn now to look briefly at the sale that goes sour - the sale that we can't finalize because we can't collect the money. It doesn't take rocket science to deduce that if a prospect doesn't pay for whatever it is that he has said he wants to buy, the problem boils down to one of two things: (1) He doesn't have the ability to pay, or (2) He has changed his mind about buying.

THE PROSPECT WHO CAN'T PAY. When you end up with a prospect who says "yes" but doesn't have the money to buy the product or service you've sold him, you have earned the right to go out and buy yourself a GS-LQ award plaque. GS-LQ, of course, stands for Great Salesperson-Lousy Qualifier. Obviously, you did a great job of selling; you got the prospect to make the buy-decision. Just as obviously, you did a lousy job of qualifying the prospect since it is now abundantly clear that he doesn't have the resources to make the purchase he has agreed to. Give yourself a nice pat on the back and a swift kick wherever you think it will do the most good.

Can you salvage anything from this situation? Maybe. The prospect's financial situation may be subject to significant change. Talk with him and address that issue head-on. Perhaps you can even serve as a consultant in that regard. Set a date on which you will check back with him to see if the sale can then be confirmed. At the very least, since you have sold him on the value of your product or service, ask him for the names of friends and/or associates who might be good prospects. He will be grateful to you for the positive way in which you have dealt with his problem and will probably do his best to supply you with some good leads.

THE PROSPECT WHO HAS CHANGED HIS MIND. It may at first be difficult to distinguish this prospect from the one just discussed, the financially embarrassed individual. But you will quickly discover when you follow-up with this prospect that the problem is not money, but motivation. He has changed his mind about buying whatever it was that he said "yes" to. You may initially have thought that he was just a slow payer. The first red flag in his case appeared when he failed to respond promptly to the bill mailed out to him from your office. Then you may have had a delicate and indirect phone conversation with him about the billing and his lack of response. He even may have given you the proverbial "The check is in the mail" line. But the one point that really matters here is that several days have passed since you made the sale, and it is still not confirmed. What that equates to, of course, is: No payment; no sale.

In order not to waste your own valuable time, you must very quickly confirm that this prospect is **able** but **doesn't choose** to buy your product/service. Some salespersons are inclined to beat around the bush with this type prospect for fear of losing a sale. But indirectness on your part only avoids facing the reality of this situation, namely, that the prospect has changed his "yes" to a "no." Unless you are able to resell this individual, the sale is already lost. If you are able to discover why the individual has changed his mind, you will have at least a chance of answering his objection(s) and closing him again.

> *Example:* A stock broker who sold a prospect a $20,000 trade five days ago has finally managed to get through to him on the phone. The broker says: "Mr. Franklin, I've been really concerned about finalizing the trade that we agreed on last week. I've checked each day with my office to see if your payment has come in. I know that you have the resources to make the trade, so I have to conclude that for some reason you've changed your mind. I need to talk with you about that because, as I explained last week in your office, this particular deal gives every indication of netting you a substantial profit. How about telling me what's come up so that I can answer any new questions you may have."

Summary

This chapter has focused on the things that the salesperson has to do in order to turn closed business into paid-for business. We call it confirming, or finalizing, a sale. It would be hard to overstate the importance of the confirming procedure. If closing is the most exciting thing that a salesperson does, then surely confirming is the most practical.

9

SELLING:
MAKING A CAREER OF IT

Introduction

If you decide to make a career out of selling, you will need to develop a philosophy - an attitude and perspective - that enables you to feel good about yourself and your chosen profession. Developing this philosophy, which is really a particular kind of outlook on life, is not a low-priority option which you can decide to deal with or not; it is a **must**, an absolute imperative, if you plan to make a career out of sales. **Without** an overarching strong and positive attitude about yourself and your "world" of prospects and customers, you will be vulnerable to every failure that comes your way and constantly pushed toward depression and despair by the stress and frustration that surround you on a daily basis. But **with** a philosophy - a general attitude and perspective - that gives value and purpose to both your personal and professional life, you will face each new day with enthusiasm and anticipation, and you will be immune to the potentially debilitating exigencies which continually confront you.

Personal Traits and Behaviors

HONESTY. In the long run it's yourself that you have to live with; it's yourself you have to be able to like. If as a salesperson you only sell products or services that you believe in, you'll have no guilt feelings to hide from or deal with. If you make only honest and forthright claims about the features and benefits of what you sell, and if you avoid using ambiguous and misleading statements in your sales presentations, you will make many sales and gain many satisfied customers. You will also build a reputation for yourself that will increase your sales. But most importantly, you will be satisfied, even pleased, with who you are as a private person and as a salesperson.

CONFIDENCE. The salesperson who believes in the **value** of what he is selling **and** in his **ability** to sell it has the two necessary ingredients for confidence. Confidence isn't something that you snatch out of thin air; nor is it something that you should hope that you can **find**. Rather, it is something that you can **grow** for yourself. Choose products or services to sell that you believe have **real** value.

Then learn all that you can about them so that you can present them intelligently and convincingly. Sales will come to you, and with them, confidence!

OPTIMISM. There is truth in the old saying that describes an optimist as one who always sees a glass that is half full, never one that is half empty. The lyric of a popular song from a previous generation instructs us to "accentuate the positive" and "de-emphasize the negative." Being optimistic really is a matter of choice. Good **and** bad things happen to everyone. Successes **and** failures come to everyone. An individual must **choose** whether to focus on positive or negative things in life.

The successful salesperson is **always** an optimist; a pessimist could not exist long-term in sales. For an optimist, a prospect's "no" is never a defeat; it is a merely an obstacle which, once gotten around, brings the salesperson one step closer to his next "yes." Optimism **expects** success, and in expecting it, helps to bring it about. An optimistic expectation often turns out to be a self-fulfilling prophecy.

ENTHUSIASM. Enthusiasm is the result of being happy about what you are doing. If you **like** what you do for a living, you will be enthusiastic about it. Your prospects and customers will **see** your enthusiasm and **respond** to it. It is a very positive and contagious thing. It is not unusual for a prospect or customer to say to a genuinely enthusiastic salesperson, "You **really like** what you are doing, don't you?" The enthusiasm of a salesperson often stimulates interest on the part of a prospect - interest that results in a sale, which in turn reinforces the salesperson's enthusiasm. Enthusiasm is a dynamic thing that tends to multiply and reproduce itself as it interacts with other people.

THANKFULNESS. Most persons take for granted many things for which they should be thankful. The positive outlook on life that every salesperson desires to develop is heightened by focusing on the specific things which most people take for granted: (1) health, (2) intelligence, (3) food and shelter, (4) family and friends, (5) a good job, (6) life in America, etc. The individual who starts a new day with a conscious awareness of how fortunate he is, in many different ways, is able to take to his work a very positive attitude.

COURAGE. As a salesperson, you will encounter good times and bad. A touch of humility will see you safely through the good times, but something more is needed for getting through the tough times. That "something more" is called courage. It's not easy to define, but it's what keeps you going when you think you can't go anymore. It's what enables you to keep "hanging on" in life when everything seems to be out of your control. Some individuals say that they are able to bolster their courage during bad times by remembering good times when they were able to "control" their lives, and by looking to the future and believing that things will be good again. Most successful salespeople are able to handle tough times by taking this **long view**. They know that they have survived hard times in the past, and they believe that they will survive the crisis of the present.

INTEGRITY. Some salespersons are like chameleons, continually changing their "colors" to match their environment. But individuals who are in sales for the long-term know that they must have a personality and character of their own; they cannot constantly transform themselves into something or someone they are not just to win the approval of a prospect. As a career salesperson, you must know **who you are**. You must **also** know **who you want to be**, that is, how you want to be **different** from the way you presently are. So, you must conduct a self-inventory in which you identify qualities that you want to shed as well as attributes that you want to develop. Once you have defined the new you, strive constantly to **be** that person. Integrity is **knowing** who you are and **always**, under **any** circumstances, **being** that person.

Strategic Traits and Behaviors

Strategic traits and behaviors have to do with successful **selling**; they are actions, habits, and techniques that the successful salesperson must develop and practice. There are two categories of these traits and behaviors: (1) Self-related, (2) Client-related.

SELF-RELATED STRATEGIC TRAITS AND BEHAVIORS. These are things that a salesperson must do by himself and for himself in order to be successful.

Motivate self. The individual who chooses to make a career out of selling must learn to keep himself motivated over the long-term. At the beginning of a salesperson's career there is usually motivation enough from a nice monthly paycheck and the daily challenges which present themselves to an individual who is new to sales. But with the passing of time many persons find themselves suffering from burnout and needing to find something that will "keep them going."

When this happens, you should take stock of your own situation and make a list of the things that are most important in your life, including the things that you have not yet attained. You should be able to come up with a half-dozen reasons why you are still working - things you want to accomplish, places you want to go, things you want to buy, obligations you want to take care of. Make a list of them and put it somewhere where you see it every day. Many persons have pictures on their desks or office walls which remind them of what they are working for - pictures of family, vacations homes in the mountain or at the beach, achievement plaques and sales awards, boats, cars, travel posters, etc. Just as you have to give a prospect a reason for buying, a motive for saying "yes," you need to keep yourself surrounded with objects and symbols that motivate you.

Manage stress. Entire books have been written about managing stress. The experienced salesperson should have an edge over most people when it comes to dealing with stress because it is a part of his daily existence. Life is filled with situations that produce stress, but most situations that generate stress **also** offer an individual the opportunity to win recognition and reward. Every appointment with every prospect has the potential for "stressing out" the salesperson. The prospect can almost always be counted on to raise objections to the sales presentation; a sales interview can always take a turn which results in an aborted sale.

But the experienced salesperson **anticipates** stress - in a sense, looks forward to it - and manages it by seeing it as his opportunity to step up to the plate and hit a game-winning home run. No professional baseball player who dreads his turn at bat as a stress-producing situation will ever succeed in the big leagues, and no salesperson who fears sales interviews because they are inherently stressful, will succeed in a sales career. It doesn't take a lot of imagination to picture an old sales pro encountering the personification of stress and hailing him with words like these: "Move over, Mister. I know your name; I know your game; but this stage belongs to me. I've come to knock 'em dead."

Deal with problems. Everyone encounters problems throughout life. People in sales have their own special problems to deal with. There is a simple 4-step approach to handling problems that works for most people. Here it is: (1) Identify the problem. (2) Don't deny its existence or try to escape it. (3) Find a solution and implement it. (4) Move forward, leaving the problem behind. The important thing is not to let a problem get in the way of and block the normal flow of your work routine and life. Usually, if faced head-on, a problem can be solved quickly. Sometimes the implementation of a solution extends over time. In either case, the sooner you put a problem behind you, allowing it either **no** place at all, or at most, a very **small** place in your ongoing life, the better off you will be.

Accept responsibility. As a salesperson you will have many successes and some failures. When you have a failure, accept the responsibility for it. **Don't blame** someone else and look for excuses. **Analyze** what happened and try to determine what you could have done differently to achieve the outcome that you wanted. **Learn** from failures and transform them into productive experiences. In some cases, of course, your analysis of a failure will show you that what happened was really caused by circumstances beyond your control. Be philosophic about such cases and move forward. Nobody can control everything all of the time.

Be open to new approaches. Career salespeople have to guard against the "Been there; done that" philosophy. You can always learn new, more effective ways to handle particular sales situations. Inexperienced salespersons make many mistakes but are usually open to trying virtually any strategy to get a sale. Experienced individuals can sometimes pick up something new (that actually works!) from a junior salesperson. Of course, everyone in sales should analyze every sales interview that they conduct, whether it is successful or not, to see what new thing(s) they can learn. In sales, as in most other areas of life, learning occurs along a linear track that runs to infinity.

Use time effectively. This is another topic on which many books have been written. The bottom line here is that there are two guidelines that should be followed in order to manage your time effectively: (1) Allocate work time to the **right** things. (2) Don't **waste** work time.

First, it doesn't matter how hard or long you work if you work on the wrong things. For example, some salespersons spend far too much time recording and filing information about prospects and customers. Only **strategic** information should be recorded and filed, that is, only information that you are **certain** to need and use in the process of selling. And **no** information should be written up and filed for a prospect that you know is "dead wood." This is just one example of how some salespeople misappropriate their work time. You must sit down and make a list of all of the work tasks that you have to deal with. Then prioritize them according to their importance and assign specific amounts of time to them as you fit them into your daily schedule. Some work tasks will get very little time, or even no time. That's O.K. The important thing is that you are committing the right amounts of time to the right tasks.

Second, work time is a precious commodity; don't waste **any** of it. If you don't already have one, make a **detailed** daily work schedule. Block in every minute of your work day. Now, look for blocks of time that are spent doing non-strategic things: coffee breaks, snack breaks, lunch, talking with colleagues, personal phone calls, personal business, reading newspapers or magazines, trips to the restroom, relaxing between phone calls and appointments, etc. Probably most of these things **must** be done during your work day, **but** are you spending too much time doing them? By minimizing the amount of time you spend on these non-strategic tasks during an average work week, you may be able to reassign several hours each week to your high-priority work tasks.

CLIENT-RELATED STRATEGIC TRAITS AND BEHAVIORS. These are things that a salesperson must do with / to / for his client in order to be successful.

Focus on client. Your prospects and customers **are** your business. Without them you are not a salesperson. Your first priority should always be to discover their needs. Having done that, you should try to meet those needs with any of your products or services that are appropriate. Successful salespeople are **always** attuned to the changing needs of their customers, and their approach to prospects is always: "Tell me about your needs;" never, "Let me tell you about what I'm selling."

Call in person. Today's salesperson uses the phone a great deal - prospecting, setting appointments, and selling. But there is no substitute for one-on-one, face-to-face selling. It allows you to build relationships with your prospects and customers. They will come to trust you and depend upon you, and they will appreciate the fact that you cared enough about them to leave your office and call on them in person.

Vary sales approach. You may talk with the same prospect on the telephone several times before you see him on an appointment. When you are talking to many prospects on the phone (perhaps **hundreds**), it is easy to fall back on a canned sales message without bothering to customize it for prospects you have called before. It's important, therefore, to make notes on prospect cards so that you will know when you are talking with an individual for the 2nd or 3rd time. That person is going to want to hear something **new** from you, not just the same canned spiel you recited to him on the previous call. You should begin a phone conversation with such a prospect in the manner of the example below:

> ***Example:*** "Fred, my records show that I spoke with you on the 14th. You were going to be out of town for a few days. I wanted to get back with you because I've got some additional information on the product we were talking about ......"

This sort of customized approach makes the prospect feel special. He knows that you talk to many people on the phone, but he senses that somehow, in spite of that, you know who **he** is.

Sell with confidence. Confidence is a trait that every salesperson must have inside himself, but it is also something that he must convey to every prospect. Communicating confidence to a prospect has mainly to do with how much and how strongly you believe in what you are selling. If you believe greatly that the product or service that you are selling is the best of its kind on the market, you will most likely **show** your conviction and confidence to your prospect as you give him your sales presentation. You communicate confidence to a prospect through both the **content** of the words you speak and the

enthusiasm with which you deliver them.

Handle customer problems head-on. You are bound to have situations occur where a customer is unhappy with a product or service that you sold him. A customer with a problem that you can fix is a great opportunity for you. Encourage him to talk about the problem. Get him to define and describe it. Give him every opportunity to convince you (and himself!) how important and significant the problem is. Then fix it for him! You will probably win a customer for life.

Some problems, of course, you won't be able to fix. You may have sold a stock whose trading price fell sharply. Or a prospect, attempting to save money, may have bought a product or service that turned out to be inadequate for his needs. In cases where you can't fix the problem yourself without cost to the customer, you can at least serve him as a consultant. Give him suggestions for solving his problem. You may have **other** products or services which **will** meet his needs. If you don't, recommend a company that does. He will appreciate your unselfish attitude and will think of you when he needs something that you **do** sell.

Resist mudslinging. You never paint a pretty picture of yourself and your company when you throw mud at competing salespersons and their companies. No matter what you are selling these days, there are lots of other salespeople selling the same thing. You don't make yourself look good by trying to make somebody else look bad. Most prospects and customers are made uncomfortable by salespersons who badmouth their competitors. Besides, the prospect you're talking with may be a good friend and customer of the salesperson you're putting down. Win customers by being a nice guy and touting the merit of your own product or service.

Avoid excessive joking and crude talk. Some prospects and customers may seem to almost **invite** you to sling some _____ with them or to match their outpouring of crude joke after crude joke. Be polite, but don't get pulled into this unprofessional arena. You don't have to be judgmental of the prospect; just don't encourage his performance or participate in it. You always have a right to be yourself. Any prospect or customer who would deny you that right is probably not a customer you need, or for that matter, **want**.

Get referrals. The successful salesperson never stops prospecting. One of the best times to get the names of new prospects is immediately after you make a sale. You've just convinced the person you're sitting down talking with that your product or service is worth buying. He just bought it! Whether you sold him a product for personal or business use, he is bound to have friends or business associates who have similar tastes. Compliment him on his good judgment in buying your product, and then take him into your confidence and use him as a consultant who can give you referrals, as in the example below.

> *Example:* "You've made a good decision, Jean. The silver flatware you just selected is very beautiful, and you'll appreciate its quality more and more with every passing year. I know you must have many friends who share your conviction that **beautiful** sterling can **also** be **affordable** and **durable**. Who among them do you think would like to see this line of silver service and flatware?"

Summary

You can be proud that you have chosen to make a career of selling. You have chosen a profession that will offer countless challenges; but the rewards that you earn for yourself, both personal and professional, will be great. Your successes will sustain you through periods of frustration and adversity, and in the end you will know that all of your efforts were "worth the doing." This book is dedicated to you, and we repeat that dedication here:

> To salespersons everywhere, whose hard work and
> productivity continue to provide business and
> industry with a reason for being.

APPENDIX:
NETWORK MARKETING

1

INTRODUCTION TO NETWORK MARKETING

Introduction

IT'S BIG. At this moment some **6 million** Americans are employed in the network marketing industry, an industry whose various companies sell products and services amounting to nearly **$60 billion annually**. Conservative business writers predict that during the 1990's as much as 60% of all goods and services sold in the U.S. will be sold through multilevel and network sales organizations. Authorities on the industry predict annual sales of **$100 billion** by the turn of the century.

IT'S THE WAVE OF THE FUTURE. The downsizing of giant corporations is no longer news. In the past three years IBM, AT&T, and General Motors have together let go 279,000 workers. Business operations that are heavy at the top where the customers are not can't hope to maintain their leadership in the consumer-sales race. Multilevel and network marketing companies that are heavy at the bottom of the organizational triangle - where the customers **are** - will become the dominant force in delivering products and services to consumers.

IT'S EVERYBODY'S OPPORTUNITY. Newspapers across the country are filled these days with stories of longtime, faithful employees who have been let go (read "**fired**") by companies that are downsizing in order to remain profitable. Corporate spokespersons have even coined pleasant sounding words to describe what is being done to thousands of employees. The workers are told that they have been "selected out," "furloughed," or given "early retirement." But euphemistic phrases don't hide for long the reality that these individuals have been **excluded** from the ranks of the employed and are now jobless and, in many cases, faced with financial disaster. By contrast, network marketing companies always have the welcome mat out. They constantly seek to be **inclusive**. Their success depends on their ability to constantly **enlarge** their sales groups.

DEFINING IT. Network marketing is a method or strategy for the retail selling of a product (or service) that encourages independent sales representatives not only to sell the product themselves, but to recruit and develop new salespersons whose sales production will result in commissions for the individuals who, directly or indirectly, recruited them. Network marketing is **not** a **pyramid scheme**. Pyramid schemes operate in similar fashion to chain letters; they generate revenue by recruiting new members and charging them admission fees. Typically they sell no product (or at least none of any significance), and frequently those who did not join early in the game lose their investment when the pyramid collapses (for lack of anything to hold it together, such as legitimate product to be sold).

EXPLAINING IT. In this chapter we will make a special effort to describe how network marketing works; but if you are a network marketer, you should not think that this is the **only** chapter in this book that you need to read! **All** of the other nine chapters have great importance for you. Topics such as "Communication," "Telephone Performance," "Developing Sources," "Prospecting and Qualifying," and "Handling Objections" are extremely relevant to your sales work. If you have not already read the eight chapters which precede this one, go back to the "Table of Contents" at the front of the book and see what you've missed. This book is for **you**, the **whole** book, not just this chapter.

The Problem With Traditional Selling

THE "LONE RANGER" APPROACH. Even the Lone Ranger had Tonto, but if you are doing traditional retail or direct selling, you have only yourself! At the end of each day and each week and each month, the one big question is: "How much did **you** sell?" We put the word "you" in boldface print because that focuses attention on the point we want to make, namely, if **you** didn't sell it, it doesn't count for you. You get credit for what **you** sell, period!

Every experienced salesperson knows the frustration that comes from putting in long hours in a store (retail sales) or on the phone or road (direct sales), and still coming up with sales production that falls short of his own and his employer's expectations. In such situations, the salesperson vows to work smarter and harder and longer, but very often, because of the incredible competitiveness of the marketplace, finds that his increased dedication and efforts result in little or no increase in his productivity. The frustration that such a situation produces is compounded by the fact that the individual sees no prospect of ever getting out of the "box" that he is presently in.

What If You Had 100's of Salespeople Working For You?

A NON-SALES ANALOGY. "EACH ONE TEACH ONE." This was the motto that inspired a humanistic organization dedicated to wiping out illiteracy on our planet earlier this century. It doesn't take a lot of analysis to comprehend that 100's and 1000's of individuals battling illiteracy can post major gains a lot faster than a single individual or even numerous individuals working through a relatively small organization. The notion that every person taught to read would as "payment" teach at least one other person to read bore great results for the organization that came up with the concept. Although the idea did not produce a geometric progression (constantly expanding multiplication) of the number of persons being taught to read, it **did** trigger a theoretically endless continuation of the battle against illiteracy.

WHAT IF YOU COULD CLONE YOURSELF 256 TIMES (AND MORE)? Would that increase your sales productivity? Here we have the concept of network marketing which we will explore in detail in this chapter. Brace yourself for the ride! Imagine a network of hundreds of salespersons whose sales earn commissions for you just because you sponsored and taught a handful of individuals at the head of a stream - **your** stream, your downline.

The New Network Marketing Philosophy

A REAL BUSINESS. Network marketing is a **real** business with major income potential. In the past, many people came into the industry not looking at it as a serious business opportunity but as a sideline venture to dabble in. Many individuals joining the industry today take a very different outlook on the whole matter, preparing a Business Plan (with short-term and long-term goals) for themselves, knowing how much they are willing to spend on a weekly basis in order to establish their "own business," and intending to be around for the "duration."

PATIENCE REQUIRED. In a traditional business the start-up cost is usually very high, often in the tens or hundreds of thousands of dollars. Reaching the break-even point on the initial investment usually requires several (perhaps many) years. Yet, historically, many persons have been willing to invest large sums of money and wait long periods of time to "get their business going." By contrast, individuals entering the network marketing industry have generally been short on patience and have often moved on to "something else" long before their minimal investment of time and money had any real opportunity to bear fruit.

Over the years network marketing companies have seen countless individuals come on board to "try it out." Typically a person will recruit a few friends without teaching them anything about the business, sell a little product, look for a big paycheck, hang-in for a few weeks, and check out of the industry before gaining any real understanding of what it is all about. Usually such persons were motivated in the first place because they either knew or had heard of individuals with big downline sales organizations and impressive residual incomes. Most new recruits to the industry seldom consider that its star performers did not rise to the top with meteoric speed, but rather, "paid dues" over many months (or several years) in order to gain the solid ground of success that they now occupy.

"GOT TO HAVE A PLAN" - BUSINESS PLAN, THAT IS. There is an old saying that declares "There is no shortcut to success." We have already seen that many newcomers to network marketing view the industry **itself** as a shortcut to success. But we have also seen what happens to them; they quickly fall by the wayside. But the fact is that there is a fast track to success in network marketing. It involves the development of a Business Plan - a strategy for launching and establishing a new business. In a general sense, a Business Plan for a network marketing enterprise is similar to such a plan for any other business, but the entrepreneur who decides to "make his fortune" in the arena of network marketing must pay special attention to two problem areas.

"DON'T LOSE 'EM." The first is the matter of **attrition** - the falling away of individuals recruited for the entrepreneur's downline. Experienced network marketers know all too well how vital it is to keep attrition at a minimum. The **concept** which drives network marketing is a fantastically powerful concept - geometric progression. It is the idea that each new individual brought into a sales organization (downline) keeps multiplying himself by 2 or 4 (or whatever). This exponential growth of an entrepreneur's downline (if each individual bought only a small amount of company product; let alone, **sold** some to other people) would very quickly make the sponsor of the downline extremely wealthy.

But, of course, each new recruit in a sponsor's downline does **not** multiply himself by 2 or 4 for an infinite number of times. All too often, the new recruit simply disappears, dropping out of the business before multiplying himself at all. In such cases the sponsor not only does not profit from the new recruit, but loses whatever time and money he invested in the individual. It is this kind of attrition that the network marketing entrepreneur wants to minimize by every possible means. One of the best ways to accomplish that is to recruit and sponsor individuals not wide, but deep. If he can sponsor 2 persons, motivating them and teaching them in ways that empower them to duplicate the process which just brought them into the organization, then he is on the right track.

But the sponsor must do more than teach the two new recruits how to recruit others; if he is to safeguard against losing them prematurely, he must show them how to make money in the short-term. If he can show them how to recruit a couple of persons and move enough product to realize almost immediate financial gain, then he will have helped them accomplish something that they will see as powerful and exciting. They will see the network marketing business as something worth working at, and they will **not** be lost to attrition.

EARNING FROM YOUR DOWNLINE. The second major concern of the entrepreneur who is devising a Business Plan for his network marketing enterprise is the matter of **residual income** - income produced for him by his downline without his personal involvement. Many of the individuals mentioned earlier as "dabblers" in network marketing would scoff at the idea that the industry can provide an "early retirement" option for those who plan and work for it. But the reality is that large residual incomes **can** be earned in the industry. They must simply be **planned** for. An individual must study his company's compensation plan and then, based on that, develop the kind of sales organization necessary to produce for him the amount of residual income that he desires. Successful strategies for producing residual income focus not just on the size of the downline, but also on sales techniques and plans which enable a limited number of persons to move a large volume of product in short periods of time.

"SHOW THEM A PROFIT." Individuals considering a career in network marketing today want to know how quickly they will be able to recoup their initial investment - the old "risks vs. rewards" concern. The entrepreneur who can convincingly demonstrate to prospects and new recruits that they can not only regain their initial investment but also realize a profit in the short-term will find that he has many "takers" for his invitation to join his business.

"YOU CAN DO IT, TOO." The genius of network marketing - its uniqueness - is based on the concept of **duplication**. If an individual can show others that he has a business strategy that works - a strategy that wins new recruits and sells product - **and** if he can convince them that **they** can duplicate that process, then he can expect to win many loyal followers, establish a productive sales organization, and secure significant residual income. But he will not be alone in the "Winner's Circle." There is a kind of built-in, self-perpetuating motivational factor in today's new network marketing equation: what's good for the entrepreneur (sponsor, leader, etc.), is good for his downline, and vice versa. A successful teacher (sponsor) produces successful followers who in turn repeat the cycle. Thus in a network marketing sales organization each individual profits from his empowering other individuals to succeed - a happy formula indeed, unique, in the business world, to the network marketing industry.

Becoming a Professional in Network Marketing: Getting Started

SELECT A COMPANY AND SIGN ON. There are many network marketing companies to choose from. Some have been around a long time; some are relatively new. With a newer company there is often a better opportunity to build a large downline beneath yourself, and of course that is a positive factor to consider with regard to (1) gaining early profit and (2) building a base for residual income. But the age of a company, considered by itself, is not as important as several other factors. Listed below are sample "due diligence" questions you should consider when choosing a company.

- Can you get excited about the products or services the company sells?
- Does it have a good compensation plan?
- Is the company's compensation and marketing plan duplicatable? For you? For those you sponsor?
- Are the products of high quality and appropriately priced? Are they asset-enhancing?
- Is there a strong consumer need for the products?
- Can a strong consumer demand be created for the products?
- Do the products have intrinsic and/or collectible value?
- Does the company provide training for sales representatives?
- Does it have good sales aids and support materials, e.g., training manual, catalogs, flyers, brochures, audio and video tapes, etc.?
- Do you understand how the company earns money?
- Is the company new or old? Is there still "room at the top"?
- Does the company have short and long-term business plans?
- Does the company employ appropriate professional advisors?
     CPA's to oversee financial record keeping?
     Lawyers to see that the company stays "regulatory right"?
     Computer specialists to coordinate information flow?
- Are financial records of company updated and published at timely intervals for the benefit of the management team and other interested parties?
- Does it have an "arms-length" professional management team with no downlines in home office or conflicts of interest?
- Do company officers have collective experience in corporate management, sales, and marketing, as well as network marketing?
- Does the company have a solid financial foundation? Strong capitalization?
- Is the company owned by its sales representatives and/or a diverse shareholder group?
- Does it offer group insurance? Life? Health?
- Does it have a good compensation program? Is a detailed explanation of how it works available to prospective sales representatives?
- How do experienced sales reps feel about the company?
- Does it have a solid financial foundation? Strong capitalization?

These are the kinds of questions you should seek answers to as you shop around for a company to commit to.

BUY YOUR COMPANY'S PRODUCTS. It's tough to sell something you don't believe in, and it's impossible to really believe in something you haven't experienced personally. So buy some of the products your company sells and get excited about them. When you're selling something to someone else, there's no testimony as effective as your own. Customers always want to know: "What do **you** think?" Whenever possible, have products with you to **show** to customers. You should understand the appeal (sizzle) that the physical presence of your products has for influencing them (both to **buy** the products themselves and to **join** your sales team). This is especially important if you are selling products that are "collectible" or wealth-building. Of course another reason for buying your company's products is that you can buy them wholesale. You can get quality products at less than retail price and build your sales production number at the same time.

Building Your Sales Organization

BECOME A SPONSOR. If there is a single most important key to the appeal and the success of network marketing, this is it! Being a sponsor is how you build your own sales organization. It is how you move a large volume of your company's product. It is how you earn money for what your downline sells. It is how your company grows and makes a profit, enabling it to serve you better with an expanded product line, better service, and more benefits.

By becoming a sponsor you are able to clone yourself, replicate yourself an infinite number of times. By becoming a sponsor you are able to beat the "Lone Ranger" approach to selling; you are able to set up a sales organization that earns for **you** at the same time it is earning for itself. As a sponsor you find yourself in the wonderful position of being the benefactor of the sales productivity of a large group of individuals motivated to work their hardest in order to best serve their own self-interest. The more they serve themselves, the more they serve you. And it's all guilt-free for you because your people can achieve the same thing you have achieved; in fact, it's to your benefit to help them do it.

CHOOSE ONLY A FEW. Most people have very distorted ideas about the recruiting that is required of individuals who are successful network marketers. They hear stories about persons who have down-line sales organizations of hundreds of people and naturally assume that the individual at the top of that group had to recruit everyone in it. Not surprisingly, these outsiders shake their heads in amazement and write off network marketing as something they could never do. Too bad they don't understand that successful network marketers sponsor only a few Front Line individuals in their sales organizations.

The U.S. Marines in a recruitment campaign a few years ago declared, "We're looking for a **few** good men!" Some people responded cynically to the slogan saying to themselves, "Yea, right, tell me another one." But the Marines aside, the individual who has recently signed on with a network marketing company really **is** looking for only a few good individuals to sponsor. Different companies have different plans and options, but almost always a new employee is encouraged to begin building his sales network by sponsoring no more than 8 persons; normally the number ranges from 2 to 8.

CHOOSE CAREFULLY. Naturally, you will want to sponsor individuals who will succeed in the business since your own success will be dependent in large measure on theirs. But who to choose? What sort of profile should you look for? You want an individual who

- has many contacts.
- likes working with other people.
- likes to show and tell others how to do something.
- wants to have his own business.
- is willing to work hard to gain freedom and financial independence.
- is naturally excited and enthusiastic about something he believes in.
- enjoys being a team player.
- is organized and likes to keep things "in order."
- is creative and likes to think of new ways to do something.
- likes to help others succeed.
- likes to plan and carry out his own work schedule.
- is a self-starter.
- is willing to invest time in the short run in order to profit financially in the long run.

A quick reading of this profile might seem to suggest the classic salesperson type, but there is a risk in sponsoring individuals who have been successful in traditional sales, especially direct sales. There are two things that the successful network marketer must be very good at doing which are altogether foreign to the traditional salesperson: (1) He must be an organization builder, and (2) He must be a teacher. We will speak of these two things at much greater length later in this chapter, but suffice it to say at this point that there is nothing in the experience or background of the traditional salesperson that would cause him to assign any value to either of these two skills which are so essential to the individual who wants to succeed in network marketing. In fact, the traditional salesperson's natural tendency would be to see both organization-building and teaching as irrelevant obstacles to be swept out of the way of what he sees as the one all-important task of every salesperson - selling.

ESTABLISH YOUR FRONT LINE. Your Front Line is made up of the few individuals whom you choose to sponsor as the foundation of your sales organization. Recall that we said earlier in this chapter that the number of Front Line positions usually ranges from 2 to 8. For the purpose of our discussion here, let's say that you decide to build a sales organization based on a Front Line of 4 positions. It is **imperative** that you fill these 4 positions with persons who, with your instruction and help, will be capable of replicating the organization-building task that you are presently engaged in.

HELP BUILD YOUR DOWNLINE. Your downline is your sales organization, your multi-level network of individuals, recruited by yourself and by those whom you recruited. Let's see what a 4-level (4-generation) downline looks like.

	You			
1st Level	01	01	01	01
2nd Level	04	04	04	04
3rd Level	16	16	16	16
4th Level	64	64	64	64
Totals	**85**	**85**	**85**	**85**
	Grand Total = 340			

You can see how quickly your organization grows by the process of replication. You sponsor 4 persons in your Front Line. Those 4 each sponsor 4 more, and so on; so that each successive level (or layer) of your downline is 4 times bigger than the preceding level. Each of your original Front Liners now has his own downline of 84 persons; and by building your sales organization just 4 levels deep, you have established a downline for yourself of 340 persons! Just to show you the incredible power of the geometric progression which is at work here, compare the numbers of persons that would appear in successive levels (up to 10) of your organization if we continued to multiply the total number in each level by 4.

4th Level	=	256
5th Level	=	1,024
6th Level	=	4,096
7th Level	=	16,384
8th Level	=	65,536
9th Level	=	262,144
10th Level	=	1,048,576

Of course these numbers are only theoretical. Everyone knows that in the real world individuals will drop out of your organization or fail to replicate themselves times 4, etc. And that is why it is so critical that you **start** your organization with 4 Front Line persons who are serious about the business and who, **with your help**, will replicate themselves times 4, and so on. It cannot be emphasized enough how important it is for you to **teach** your Front Liners so that they will be both **motivated** and **capable** of duplicating the acts of recruiting and sponsoring that you have just done with them. The **key** to building a large downline for yourself is doing everything in your power to help your Front Liners build the top 3 levels of **their** downlines with quality people. Remember, their people are your people!

One thing to remember when you are building your downline: it won't happen overnight. It takes a lot of hard work and time. If you can get the first 3 levels of your sales organization in place and have them functioning effectively in 6 months, you can be really proud of your efforts.

Maintaining Your Sales Organization

REPLACE DEADWOOD IN YOUR DOWNLINE. We have just looked at the impressive numbers generated by the principle of geometric progression which gives such a dramatic boost to your organization-building efforts. But you need to be fully aware of the fact that in the real world your downline will not develop in a perfectly uniform way. It's growth will be slowed by "breaks and bruises" that occur all too frequently. In spite of your very best efforts to advise and direct them, **your** Front Liners will make mistakes in choosing some of **their** Front Liners, and **their** first-level people will do the same thing. But the slowed growth of your sales organization will not always be the result of someone choosing and sponsoring a "wrong" person; in some cases a "right" person will have to put his commitment to network marketing on a back burner due to unforeseen circumstances that suddenly demand all of his time and concentration.

The point is that in no time at all you will have deadwood in your downline; and that is a very bad thing, especially if it occurs in the first 3 levels of your organization. It is such an important thing that some poetically inclined network marketer would do the industry a great service by writing a little fun (but **serious**!) verse bearing the title: "Look Out for Deadwood in Your Downline." So...... Why not?

Look out for deadwood in your downline;
It'll thwart your efforts in no time.
Clear it out and throw it away;
Make a path for a brighter day.
Look out for deadwood in your downline;
It'll kill your business in no time.

So, it is very important to work with your Front Line people and **their** Front Line people to plug holes in your developing sales organization. There is an old saying that says, "A stitch in time saves nine." There is **profound** truth in this saying for the network marketer. A **single** deadwood individual in the first 3 levels of your downline can have a **huge** negative impact on your organization. Look at the chart above and see!

Expanding Your Sales Organization

MANAGE YOUR GROWTH. Most authorities agree that an individual should never have more than 8 Front Liners with whom he is working actively at any one time. Some argue that 4 should be the maximum number. Experience, of course, makes a difference, and some individuals who like to "live and breathe" network marketing may have no trouble managing twice as many first-level positions as a newcomer to the industry. In any case, remember that managing a Front Liner means working down-group with him, helping him manage the 2 or 3 levels directly below him. Never spread yourself too thin. If you are responsible for too many Front Liners at the same time, you will not be able to work down-group with them, and the result will be that the levels immediately beneath your Front Liners will be chaotic and non-productive. Always remember that helping those below you (in your sales organization) achieve **their** goals is the surest way to guarantee that you will achieve your **own** goals..

Teaching the People in Your Sales Organization

AN ANALOGY ABOUT A HOUSE. We have just talked about building, maintaining, and expanding your sales organization. Intentionally we focused on the **structure** or mechanics of the organization. We talked about what it **looks** like - how big it is, how it fits together, how its different parts relate to one another. In a way, what you've just experienced might be compared to being given a tour of a great mansion with hundreds of rooms. A guide tells you all about the architectural design of the house; he shows you many of the rooms and the hallways and stairways that connect them; he tells you about the wiring and plumbing and the heating and cooling required by the mansion. But you have questions that the guide has not answered. You want to know who built the house and why. You want to know who lived there and what they did. You want to know the **human** story of the house. And that's just what we are coming to now with regard to our explanation of network marketing - the human side of the story.

TEACH YOUR COMPANY'S STORY. Your company has a story, and you will have to tell it countless times. Whenever you meet with prospects, whenever you talk with your Front Liners, whenever you work with downline sales representatives, you will tell some part (if not all) of your company's story. You will tell who your company is - who its leaders and officers are. You will tell its history - how it came into being, and what it has achieved since it was organized and launched. You will do your best to make your company **personal** and human to all of the people you come in contact with. You know how important your company's story is because you understand that people **join** organizations that they feel familiar and comfortable with.

Of course you are not altogether on your own when it comes to telling your company's story. Most network marketing companies have audio and video tapes which do a good job of introducing the company to the uninitiated. And often company officers can be scheduled to speak to district and regional meetings. Finally, don't forget that you can always get help from upline; your sponsor (or your sponsor's sponsor, etc.) can always be brought in to speak to a group of your prospects and / or sales representatives.

TEACH YOUR COMPANY'S PRODUCT (OR SERVICE). No one gets any money for their efforts in network marketing if product is not sold! If product doesn't move, the company gets no revenue. That's how important product is! The company **exists** to sell product. But we will talk about **selling** in the next section of this chapter. Here, we simply want to emphasize how important it is to teach your Down-Line about product. Persons who understand product, persons who believe in the value of product, will buy it themselves (wholesale) and sell it to others (retail). **There are two things that you absolutely must teach your people about; product is one of them.**

Again, your company no doubt has an abundance of information about its product available in several formats - print (flyers, brochures, catalogs, etc.), and audio and video cassettes. Use these resources at every opportunity. If your sales organization doesn't know about or believe in your company's product, they won't buy it and they won't sell it, in which case all of your recruiting and sponsoring was for nothing! Nobody gets paid for having an organization in place. People get paid when product moves, and it moves when they know about it and believe in it.

TEACH YOUR COMPANY'S MARKETING PLAN AND SALES ORGANIZATION. Every network marketing company's marketing plan is to sell large quantities of product through its multilevel network of sales representatives. In that broad sense one company's plan is pretty much like another's. But there are many differences from company to company in terms of how the details of the industry's global (generic) marketing plan are conceived and implemented by any particular company. Naturally, some companies are more effective and productive than others in designing and carrying out their own special, customized marketing plans. The bottom line, though, in the network marketing industry is that a company's multilevel network of sales representatives **is** its marketing plan. That is to say, the

structure of a company's sales organization **is its marketing plan**.

The point here is that you must teach everyone in your downline (or **see** that they are taught) the supreme importance of the multilevel structure of your company's sales organization (as illustrated in the chart which appears earlier in this chapter). All of your people must be taught the importance of this structure so that they will (1) replicate it as they build their own downline and (2) teach its importance and the need for its further replication to the individuals they recruit for their **own** sales organizations.

Any individual who is not taught the importance of your company's marketing plan (or structure) becomes a prime candidate for not replicating himself (even **once**, let alone X 4) and at any moment may deposit himself (like a dead possum on the road) smack dab in the middle of your downline, a dead-end short circuit right where you needed it least! **The second of the two things that you must absolutely teach your people about is your company's marketing structure.**

Earlier in this chapter we said that there is a risk in sponsoring persons who have considerable experience in direct sales. This is a good place to explain why that is the case. An experienced salesperson might come into your downline and recruit like crazy. But if he fails to teach his recruits the importance of the company's multilevel sales structure and the necessity for "keeping it going," then he would **fill** your downline organization with dead-end roadblocks.

TEACH YOUR COMPANY'S COMPENSATION PLAN. There may be a rare exception to the rule here and there, but most people work to earn money. Your response to this universally known fact will probably be: "Tell me something I didn't already know." Well, one thing that the people you are recruiting for your business don't already know is your company's compensation plan. Undoubtedly it is a good one, or you would be working for a different company. The truth is, though, that most network marketing companies have fairly complicated compensation plans; or at least they **seem** complicated to someone new to the industry. So, since your company's plan is probably "something to brag about," and since the individuals you're trying to recruit don't know about it, **tell** them. Explain it in detail, and use it as a selling point to recruit new people.

The fact is that you will be better able to sell your company's compensation plan to the people you are recruiting if you have **first** customized it to fit your own special sales strategy that is a part of your personal Business Plan. If **you** already have the compensation plan working for yourself, you will be able to showcase for your recruits (1) the earnings you have reaped from it, and (2) the strategy by which you have **used** the company's plan to your benefit. All that remains for you to do is to demonstrate how your recruits can duplicate your effective use of the compensation plan for themselves.

Selling Your Company's Product (or Service)

SELL IT TO "YOUR OWN." Some of you who read this chapter will think that we have "saved the hardest thing till last," but that's not the case. In network marketing, if you play the game correctly, selling is not hard at all; in fact, it almost happens "naturally." Many experts on multilevel sales organizations insist that selling should take place as the natural result of an individual's building his sales organization, his downline.

Very early in this chapter when we were discussing becoming a part of the network marketing industry, we said that the first thing you should do after joining a company is to buy and use its products. Later, just a few paragraphs ago, we discussed the importance of teaching your sales group about your company's product. Now we bring it all together - the thinking (or philosophy) about selling product in the network marketing industry.

If you refer back to the chart that illustrates 4 levels of an individual's sales organization or downline, you will be instantly reminded of how impressive the numbers are. Just **one** of your Front Line persons with 3 levels beneath him represents 85 individuals, 85 sales reps. Think how much they can **sell** for you! Sell, indeed. Think how much they can **buy** for you. Ah, there's the secret! If you have done your job well, if you have **bought** and used company product yourself, if you have **shared** it with your recruits and required them to share it with theirs, if you have **taught** your people the value and importance of product, then you **already have** a huge amount of product flowing through your own sales organization.

Now it becomes crystal clear how important your sales organization is, how important your downline is. It is your first, probably your largest, and certainly your most enduring market for the sale of company product. **We call it selling to "your own."**

Now a **second** reason why traditional salespersons are a risky lot for you to deal with **also** becomes crystal clear. If you sponsor an individual with years of experience in direct sales, his natural inclination will be to sell, sell, sell the company's product, but odds are that he will do **that** at the expense of neglecting to build a sales organization beneath himself. As a result, his sales productivity for you will be of the flash-in-the-pan variety because as soon as he tires of selling the "same old product," he will move on to what he sees as more interesting, if not greener, "pastures." Meanwhile, you will be left with a **hole** in your downline, thanks to the itinerant sales whiz who was certain that selling a "ton" of your company's product would be "no problem." The problem is what **you** get for taking a chance and sponsoring him.

SELL IT TO FRIENDS AND RELATIVES OF "YOUR OWN." We have just pointed out the fantastic market that your own sales group provides for the sale of company product. Now we carry that idea just one step farther; we consider the market made up of the friends and relatives of your downline organization. We referred just a moment ago to the fact that each one of your 4 Front Liners heads a group of 85 sales reps (counting himself and just 3 levels beneath himself). You have 4 Front Liners, so that comes to 340 people. Surely each one of the 340 has a total of (Let's be very conservative) 3 friends and relatives to whom he could sell product. That being the case, the friends and relatives of your 3-level sales group offer up an additional 1,020 souls to whom product can be sold. And this "sell" should not be hard; in fact, it should be easy. These 1,020 potential customers are **close**, even related, to your sales group. Once again we see the value of the multilevel sales organization; it provides its own "inside" market for company product.

SELL IT TO OTHERS. Your company will have various plans for selling product to consumers outside the company, but **always** one part of any such plan will be to bring the buyers into the company's sales group. You should see clearly by now how the never-ending growth of the multilevel sales network moves an ever-increasing volume of product for the company. There are many things that you can do to bring new people into your circle of product users; some important ones are listed below.

- Talk about your product with people at every opportunity. Your enthusiasm can be persuasive.
- Sell from the heart; your passion will convince disbelievers.
- Invite new people to Business Opportunity Meetings.
- Advertise your product and company using company-approved materials.

Guidelines for Career Network Marketers

The guidelines below will help you stay on the "high road" to success in network marketing. They will also help you to avoid some common pitfalls that all too often stifle the productivity of good people who have great potential.

- Keep a positive mental attitude.
- Stay focused on projects; be persistent.
- Be patient; in 6 months you can build a whole new life.
- Take advice from experienced associates and company officials; don't try to

reinvent the wheel.
- Don't "jump" companies; pick a good one and stay with it.
- Think big; have an ambitious business plan and work to make it happen.
- Don't keep company with pessimists; they like "to rain" on other persons' "parades."
- Like selling; it's the road to independence and freedom.
- Know when to "cut your losses" with an individual who doesn't respond.
- Build a reputation for being honest and responsible; being a "good guy" pays dividends.
- Avoid the "politics" of downline competition.
- Don't "put down" other companies and their people; stay positive and promote the professional image of your own company and the industry.
- Use your sponsor and other upline persons.
- Keep a record of things that work for you, and do (or use) them again.
- Always follow up on all of your new sponsorships and sales to reinforce the other person's motivation.
- Have a modern office; be able to Fax brochures and sales information on demand.
- Take advantage of other persons' experience; use three-way calls and upline selling.
- Be a team player; share prospect referrals upline and downline; everybody benefits from cooperative efforts.
- Take advantage of company-produced materials - audios, videos, training and sales materials; use them.
- Be generous with your associates; you will get more back than you gave.
- Develop teaching methods that work and then duplicate them in the future.

A Model for Considering Network Marketing

When you consider a career in network marketing, three of the most important issues that you should focus upon are: (1) researching the industry as a whole **and** the particular company that you are thinking of joining, (2) contemplating the importance of building a downline sales organization (and how you would do it), and (3) creating a Business Plan for yourself so that you will have a strategy for success from the beginning (rather than just "winging" it). The outline below suggests points of focus that should receive your attention. Don't forget that your potential (or actual) sponsor would be a great person with whom to discuss points from this outline.

I. Conduct Research (Perform "Due Diligence")

A. Investigate Network Marketing Industry

1. Definition
2. Size
3. Trends
4. Regulatory Issues
5. Distinguish from Pyramid Organizations
6. New Improved Image

B. Investigate Different Companies
   1. Corporate History
      a. When formed or established
      b. Where incorporated
   2. Type of Business Entity (Corporation)
      a. Publicly traded
      b. Privately held
      c. Shareholder structure
      d. Subsidiaries / associated companies
   3. Management Team
      a. Corporate experience
      b. Network Marketing experience
   4. Professional Staff
      a. Legal
      b. Accounting
      c. Computer specialists
   5. Capitalization Plan
   6. Business Plan
   7. Advisory Board
   8. Policies and Procedures
   9. Expansion Plans
      a. National
      b. International

C. Investigate Products Being Sold
   1. Value
      a. Quality
      b. Uniqueness
      c. Consumability
      d. Collectibility (a wealth-building or value-based product)
   2. Market
      a. Buyer profile
         i. Gender
         ii. Age
         iii. Socio-economic groups
         iv. Ethnic/national groups

3. Competitiveness
   a. Appeal / sizzle
   b. Pricing
   c. Availability
      i. Inventory stock
      ii. Quick turnaround on orders
   d. Guarantee
   e. Return policy
4. New Products (Expansion of product lines)
   a. Type of products
   b. When available
5. Knowledge required to sell products
   a. Technical
   b. Non-technical
   c. Sources for obtaining knowledge
6. Sources of products being sold
   a. External sources
      i. Manufacturers
      ii. Distributors
   b. Internal source
      i. Company produces own products

D. Investigate Compensation Plans
   1. Types of plans
      a. Binary / Bilateral (Balanced, Self-Adjusting)
      b. Breakaway
      c. Australian Coding (Two-Up)
      d. Matrix
   2. Features to note
      a. Monthly / weekly payouts
      b. Number of levels which "count"
      c. Income potential
      d. Quotas
      e. "Flushing" volume
      f. "Bonus Volume" for product
   3. Compensation
      a. Override commissions
      b. "Leader" bonuses
      c. "Development" certificates
      d. Retail profit

E. Investigate the Timing of Your Decision to Join a Particular Company
   1. Consider stage of company's growth and development

    a. Level of opportunity for newcomers
        i.   High
        ii. Moderate
        iii. Low
2. Consider amount of time you can commit to starting your business
    a. More than what the company recommends
    b. About the same as what the company recommends
    c. Less than what the company recommends

F. Investigate Training and Sales Support Provided by Company
  1. Training program
     a. One-time shot
     b. Ongoing
  2. Training materials
     a. "Business Career Kit" (Starter Packet)
     b. Training manual
     c. Audio-Visual materials
  3. Training meetings
     a.. Local meetings conducted by sponsors, leaders, et al.
     b. Regional meetings put on by company
  4. Sales materials
     a. Catalogs
     b. Brochures, flyers, etc.
     c. Audio and/or video tapes
  5. Sales meetings
     a. Local
     b. Regional
  6. Technical support for training and sales
     a. Internet
     b. IDCC
     c. "Fax on Demand" (Sales Materials)
     d. Conference calls

II. Develop A Downline (Build Your Sales Organization)

A. Prospect
  1. Work Prospect Sources
     a. Friends and neighbors
     b. Relatives
     c. Business Associates
     d. Church and Club Contacts
     e. Persons Who Respond to Your Ads
     f. Persons Who Attend Network Events

2. Write Prospect Lists
   a. Prioritize Names

B. Recruit
   1. Use Company's Nationwide Conference Calls
   2. Use Company "Fax on Demand" Marketing Pieces
   3. Use Company Sales Aid Tools
      a. Audio-video tapes
      b. Slide shows
      c. Printed materials
   4. Use Company Meetings
      a. Local
      b. Regional
   5. Educate Rather Than Sell
   6. Anticipate Prospect's Questions and Concerns
      a. Put yourself in prospect's shoes

C. Teach Team-Building Concept
   1. Get Maximum Participation
      a. Work upline / downline
      b. Work sidelines
   2. Capitalize on Human Diversity
      a. Work backgrounds
      b. Ethnic / national backgrounds
      c. Personal life-experience backgrounds
   3. Facilitate Communication Upline and Downline
      a. Ask questions
      b. Exchange stories
      c. Discuss the business
         i. Leaders and sponsors
         ii. New recruits
   4. Create Momentum
      a. Share talents
      b. Share projects

III. Develop A Business Plan (Formulate Your Strategy For Achieving Success)

A. Major Goals
   1. Build a Productive Downline (Sales Organization)
   2. Decrease Attrition Rate
   3. Create Residual Income

B. Implementation

1. Build Depth (Not Width)
2. Use "2 X 2" Building Strategy
3. Motivation
   a. Receive Products
   b. Earn Commissions
4. Risk vs. Return
   a. Breakeven
5. How To Get Started

C. Rewards
   1. Financial Independence
   2. Personal Time Management

Thinking about and working through this outline should be extremely helpful to you as you deal with the question of making a career for yourself in network marketing. Be sure that you take advantage of the opportunity to gather input from your sponsor, other experienced salespersons in the company, and even company officials. All of them will be glad to share their knowledge and experience with you. After all, network marketing is a team thing. Your success will be their success. They **want** you to succeed!

Summary

This chapter has presented a general introduction to network marketing. It has attempted to define and describe the industry as it *really is* in the 90's - a dynamic, expanding, exciting industry that offers huge opportunity to those individuals who come to it as professionals committed to the long-term. The two chapters which follow this one will explain the sequence of steps which must be taken in order to become a successful sales representative with a network marketing company.

If you are *already* a part of, or if you are *considering* becoming a part of the network marketing industry, you may want to read the chapters in this appendix more than once. They will be very helpful to you. But it is very important for you to read this *whole* book. You should turn back to the "Table of Contents" and take note of the topics covered in the book's nine other chapters. As you no doubt know, network marketing is a special kind of sales, but it is *not* unrelated to other kinds of selling. You can profit *greatly* from reading the rest of this book. For example, knowing how to (1) communicate effectively, (2) develop new sources for prospects, (3) qualify them, (4) set up and handle an appointment, (5) deal effectively with a prospect's objections, (6) close a prospective customer - all of these are skills that *every* salesperson needs in order to be successful. These skills and techniques, and many more, are covered in the *other* chapters of this book. Commit yourself to reading and studying them with the same intensity that you will give to the three chapters on network marketing. You will *profit* from it!

2

Getting Started in Network Marketing

Welcome to the world of network marketing. As a new Independent Retail Sales Representative, you have put yourself in the right industry at the right time! Network marketers worldwide, more than 12 million strong, will sell in excess of $30 billion in product this year. This chapter is designed to make your career move a **winning** move, and get you off to a fast and productive start. You are in business **for** yourself now, but **not by** yourself. The company you have chosen to work with will stand ready to help you through each step of your new career because your success is their success. They want you to win!

What You Must Bring to Your New Business

DESIRE.

There's an old saying, "You can lead a horse to water, but you can't make him drink." It is relevant to your situation as a new sales rep in the network marketing industry. We can show and tell you how to be successful, but success will never come your way unless you **want** it, unless you have a burning desire for it. If you are satisfied with the place where you are at this point in your life, if you are complacent about the things that you already have in life and the degree of success that you have already achieved, then you are not likely to become a winner in network marketing. There must be a **gap** - a distance - between where you **now are** in life and where you **want to be** in order for you to be a strong candidate for success in network marketing. **Desire** can get you **across** that gap; desire can go a long way toward making you a phenomenal success in network marketing.

PERSISTENCE.

An older generation than ours taught its youngsters about the evils of being "a quitter." Today we tell our children (and ourselves) about the importance of "hanging tough." But it really doesn't matter much what you call it, the **value** and **importance** of the character trait that enables an individual to endure and survive good times and bad, success and failure, is impossible to overestimate. If you have the toughness and durability of character to persist at goals that you set for yourself, there is a **huge** likelihood that you will succeed in network marketing.

TEACHABILITY.

Your new business is different from anything you have done before, regardless of your personal or professional background. That is not to say that your past experience will not be helpful in your new career. But it **is** to say that you must be **open to learning** your new business fully and **correctly** from the very day you sign on. Come to the company you have chosen with a willingness and eagerness to accept techniques and procedures that have been incredibly successful for veteran network marketers.

The 9 Steps to Success

Many individuals enter network marketing with the idea that they will "give it a try and see what happens." They have heard a friend's "success story" and think that "If he can do it, so can I." But they are not prepared to work really hard at their new business. They work in "fits and starts," going "full speed ahead" for a short time and then doing nothing. In a word, they treat their new business like a hobby - something they can pick up and lay down at will. Too late they discover that if you treat a business like a hobby, it will respond like a hobby. A business must be treated like a business, worked at seriously and consistently, then it will respond like a business, repaying its diligent owner in full measure for all that he has invested in it. The **9 Steps to Success** describe how you should approach your new network marketing business. Study them carefully, and then go full blast for an exciting and richly rewarding career!

STEP #1.
STUDY YOUR COMPANY'S "CAREER KIT."

Study thoroughly all of the material in the orientation package given to you by your employer. Learn your company's "Policies and Procedures" and its "Compensation Plan." Study all forms, sales aides, and marketing materials. Comprehend the many advantages offered by your own network marketing business such as: no start-up capital required, no employee problems, no ongoing overhead cost, no advertising budget, flexible work schedule, financial independence, infinite variety of stimulating interpersonal contacts, your own sales organization, etc. etc.

STEP #2.
SIGN "LETTER OF AGREEMENT".

Accurately complete and review the "Independent Retail Sales Representative Agreement," familiarizing yourself with the responsibilities and benefits of the contract. Then sign and mail it to the appropriate office of your company.

Step #3.
Develop Contact List.

Before you talk with anyone about your new business or products, create a Contact List of at least 100 people. Ultimately the list should include all the people you know - friends, neighbors, relatives, work and business associates, people you do business with, individuals you know through civic, religious, and fraternal organizations, etc. You must put these names on paper; **it is not enough** to just "think" of a lot of people you know. And **do not** try to evaluate or gauge the value of names as you think of them. **Just put them on the list!** This Contact List is the starting point of your business.

It is not important at this point whether you are planning to work your business full-time or part-time. It does not matter whether you intend only to retail products yourself, develop a full-blown sales organization to market them for you, or both. The point is that the network marketing business is a **distribution** business. You distribute products by simply sharing their availability with people you know. Your Contact List **is** the people you know!

Do not prejudge anyone on your Contact List. Do not try to determine in advance who will be interested in your products or business. You have **products** to sell, and you have a **business** to sell. Your task is to simply **share**, in a professional and pleasant manner, your products and business with people you know. Naturally, the more people you share the products and business with, the more success you will have.

As you "grow" in the business, and if you decide to develop your own sales organization, you will use your Contact List as a source for building your downline. You will look for individuals who, in addition to possessing the necessary traits of desire, persistence, and teachability, also display a strong work ethic and leadership qualities. Keeping your Contact List current and updated will make it an invaluable tool for you in both selling and recruiting. At the end of this chapter you will find Worksheets "A" and "B" to help you develop your Contact List.

Step #4.
Develop Strong Belief-Level..........

To succeed in your new career you must develop and maintain a strong belief-level in (1) the network marketing industry, (2) your own company, and (3) yourself. You will **never** lack confidence or enthusiasm when you are sharing your products and business with people you know if your own belief in what you are doing is rock-solid. **Knowledge** is the key to a strong belief-level.

In the Industry.

Discover the facts about network marketing in the 90's. It is the most exciting and dynamic thing that is happening in sales today! Worldwide it has become a major marketing strategy. Many "Fortune 500" companies now use network marketing structures to distribute their products. You will encounter some individuals who have negative ideas about the industry, but their skepticism is rooted in a very outdated, dinosaur concept of what network marketing is all about. It's your responsibility to bring them up to date - to the threshold of the 21st century. The industry is growing and evolving so fast that you have to read current issues of business magazines (like *Success* and *Entrepreneur*) in order to keep up with what's happening, but it's well worth your effort because it strengthens your own belief-level as well as providing you with powerful facts and stories to share with your prospects and associates.

IN YOUR OWN COMPANY

Achieving a very strong belief-level in your company should be easy just as soon as you familiarize yourself with the facts about its structure, growth, products, services, and compensation plan.

IN YOURSELF.

Achieving and maintaining a strong belief-level in yourself should be the natural result of your having developed real confidence in your company and the industry of which it is a part. After all, you are **not** the Lone Ranger. You have friends, **successful** friends, who want you to succeed because **your** success is **their** success. That's how it is in network marketing; it is a joint-stock world in which your sponsor and upline associates benefit from **your** achievements just as **you** benefit from the performance of the persons in your own downline. All you have to do is keep on **sharing** (Don't think of it as **selling**) your products and business with the people on your Contact List. You will be amazed at how many positive responses you get.

And don't be concerned about the "No's" that you get because network marketing, like all sales, is a **percentage business**. Getting a "Yes" from 1-out-of-10 or even 1-out-of-20 of the persons you share your products and business with is fantastic because - **Remember**, in network marketing each person who says "Yes" to the presentation of your business becomes a part of **your** sales organization. You're **not** a stand-alone sales rep. In fact, by the end of your first year in the business you'll most likely have hundreds of individuals in your sales downline. (Go back to the previous chapter and look again at the section on "Building Your Sales Organization" to see how the numbers in your downline multiply by geometric progression.)

STEP #5.
PUT GOALS ON PAPER.

Setting goals for yourself and your new business is an absolutely essential part of the planning you must do if you want to be successful. Thinking about goals is one thing; putting them down on paper is another. Writing your goals on paper makes them tangible. You can (and must!) look at them every day. They become your "Marching Orders." They take on a reality of their own. They exist **outside** your brain. They confront you from the bulletin board above your desk (or from your refrigerator door) and pronounce judgment on your performance to date. They become a measuring stick by which you can evaluate the progress you are making in your new business.

You need to state your goals in **dollars** and **time**. You must decide how much money you want to earn from your business in certain time-frames. How much money do you want to make your 1st month? 2nd month? 3rd month? 6th month? Cumulatively by the end of the 6th month? By the end of the 1st year? Etc. If you don't tie earning levels to specific time periods, you allow yourself to work outside the discipline that comes from a sense of urgency.

Once you have a clear vision of your short-term and long-term goals, you should write them into a Business Plan that schedules the activities that must be accomplished in order to achieve specified daily, weekly, monthly, and yearly goals.

Be realistic on the conservative side in setting your goals.   There is a psychological plus that comes from under-promising and over-producing. You can "shoot for the moon" **after** you have the confidence and security that come from having repeatedly achieved the goals that you set for yourself.

STEP #6.
COMMIT FOR A YEAR.

Thousands of people stay at a job for several (often **many**!) years even though that job provides them with little money and much frustration. They rationalize their sedentary behavior by saying that at least they have "security." Of course, in **these** days of corporate downsizing, few jobs, even of the least rewarding type, offer any guarantee with regard to future employment. So, it is more the wonder that in network marketing many individuals are reluctant to "stay the course" even for 90 days, let alone a whole year. Since network marketing offers so **much** to the person who will give it a fair chance (financial independence, flexible work schedule, etc.) it is an amazing thing that it is so difficult to get new recruits to understand that committing to the development of their own business for one year is a very small price to pay for all that is to be gained. Entrepreneurs who invest in traditional business enterprises rarely expect to make a profit before the end of the second or third year. So, all of this is simply to say, "You **must** commit to your new business for a period of one year." Truth be told, many Independent Retail Sales Representatives find that they are doing "quite well" after just 90 days.

Many experienced sales reps ask their new people to commit to one "briefing" per week for 90 days **with a guest**. That means that the new rep is responsible for bringing 12 or 13 people to meetings conducted by his sponsor or other upline associate during a 3-month period. Some group leaders ask their new reps to "make two contacts a day for their business for the next 30 days." Any way you cut it, network marketing is an "exposure business." You succeed by sharing your company's business and its products with people you know. The more people you can expose to your business, the faster it will grow. So it only makes sense that you must commit yourself to **staying** with your business for a reasonable period of time - **one year**.

STEP #7.
RECOGNIZE AND USE "TOOLS" OF THE BUSINESS.

YOUR COMPANY'S "CAREER KIT."
We mentioned earlier in this chapter the importance of studying all of the materials contained in this kit. You should understand, however, that the documents in your company's orientation package are not things to be read once and then forgotten about; they should be read many times and searched for information that will help you grow your business. It goes without saying that after you have 3 months or 6 months in the business you will find information and advice in these documents that takes on a whole new meaning for you as compared to when you read it as a brand new Independent Retail Sales Representative.

Remember, too, that the book you are reading right now, *Gettin' the Business*, contains a wealth of information that can help you build and maintain your business. Read it several times, and then use it as a reference work. For example, if you begin to run out of prospects, pick up this book and reread the chapters on developing sources and prospecting. If you find that you're not as effective as you'd like to be in answering the objections of prospects, pick up the book and reread the chapter on handling objections, etc., etc.

YOUR COMPANY'S SALES AND MARKETING MATERIALS.
Your company has produced product catalogs, demonstration charts, slide sets, audio and video tapes, and a host of other sales aids. Not using these materials to the fullest possible extent is like a person who suffers hunger pangs but refuses to eat while sitting at a banquet table loaded with a wonderful variety of food.

LOCAL AND REGIONAL TRAINING SYMPOSIUMS.
Your company has many highly successful individuals who possess a vast wealth of sales and network marketing experience. By attending local and regional training sessions you can profit substantially from the ideas and experience of

others. These meetings also provide a forum for questions and answers. There is much to be gained by interacting with fellow sales reps and leaders in the company.

Local Meetings, Luncheons, and Training Sessions.

Local meetings give you a chance to learn from your sponsor and to interact with other Independent Retail Sales Representatives as well as prospects and customers. If you happen to live where there are no local meetings, you can be proactive and set up your own. Your sponsor, your upline associates, and the company's home office will be glad to help you get started.

3-Way Calls and 2 x 2 Training.

The 3-way call is an effective way to influence individuals you are trying to recruit. By adding "3-way calling" to your phone service you can enlist the help of your sponsor or some other upline person to help you tell your company's story to an interested prospect. 2 x 2 training is another technique that gives you the benefit of your sponsor's experience and expertise. After you have recruited (with the help of your sponsor) the two key persons for your new sales organization, your sponsor will help you train them so that they can, in turn, each recruit two new persons. This 2 x 2 (or 2 **train** 2) training is at the heart of how in network marketing an individual is able to duplicate (actually **multiply**) himself.

Your Company's Products.

Don't forget that one of your best business "tools" is your product line. If you can merely arrange to share your products with prospective customers, you will be amazed at the success that will come to you.

Step #8.
Maintain Consistent, Focused Activity.

Activity is work; it is action. It goes without saying that your new business will not amount to much if you don't keep working it. You must be relentless in continually, consistently pushing forward with your entrepreneurial undertaking. No business moves forward if its owner works in spurts, intermittently working hard, then laying back. This is especially true in network marketing. Momentum is required to build a sales organization, a downline; and if your work effort is sporadic rather than consistent, you will constantly be losing whatever momentum you have gained. Sporadic work effort is a lot like trying to build a bonfire during a rain shower. Throwing on a stick or two every few minutes won't win out against the falling rain. But it **can** be done. If you're willing to work really hard, without laying back and taking a break, you can build a blazing fire right in the face of the storm shower. And while it may seem like a hard pull at the moment, keep in mind that it's not going to keep on raining forever. Think what a fire you'll have **then**, when the rain stops! It's just that way with building a sales organization in network marketing. You must be **consistently active**.

But your activity, your work, must be **focused**. You must do the **right** work. As they say, you must **work smart**. You must stay busy doing the right activities. 95% of your work time should be spent doing the following things:

- Sharing Your Products
- Sharing Your Business
- Attending Company Meetings (Training Sessions, Promotional Mtgs., etc.)
- Building/Recruiting Attendance for Company Meetings

At the end of this chapter you will find Worksheet "C" which is designed to help you share your business and its products with prospects from your Contact List.

STEP #9.
CREATE LEADERSHIP.

You create leadership in others by being a leader yourself. Some key traits of leadership are listed below:

- **ACCEPT RESPONSIBILITY FOR YOUR BUSINESS.** Adopt the attitude: "My business works because of me," or "It doesn't work because of me."
- **HOLD YOURSELF TO HIGH STANDARDS.** Ask yourself: "Would I hire myself tomorrow based on the work I did today?"
- **LEAD BY EXAMPLE.** You must set the pace for your associates. They will pattern their behavior after what you do, not after what you say.
- **HELP THE PEOPLE IN YOUR SALES ORGANIZATION SUCCEED.** That is the way you succeed. Their success guarantees yours.

Summary

Naturally, a single chapter can only sketch with broad brush strokes the steps that a new Independent Retail Sales Representative must take in order to succeed with his new business. Successful network marketing entrepreneurs never fall asleep in the saddle of success. They always have their eye on the horizon, looking for new people and new ideas, but they never ignore or take for granted the turf under their feet. They understand that their business, like all business, is constantly changing, constantly in need of fine-tuning. Network marketing is a dynamic business and is managed best by a strong hand that is decisive, but sensitive. The most successful individuals learn new things everyday, from upline and downline alike, and they are smart enough and bold enough to give new ideas a try.

But having said all of this, the "basics" remain with us and are steps that all network marketers must take and never lose sight of. Here they are one more time for your review:

1 - **Study "Career Kit."**
2 - **Sign Agreement with Company**
3 - **Develop Contact List**
4 - **Develop Strong Belief-Level**
5 - **Put Goals on Paper**
6 - **Commit for a Year**
7 - **Recognize and Use "Tools" of the Business**
8 - **Maintain Consistent, Focused Activity**
9 - **Create Leadership**

Developing a "Contact List"

Who Do You Know?

Who . . .

is on your holiday card list
do you write checks to
is on your wedding list
owes you a favor
would you like to help
do you work with
does your spouse work with
have you done business with
attends your church
writes you letters
plays games with you
cleans your carpets
is from your old job
is from school/college
is from civic activities
is our favorite waiter/waitress
is from the health club
travels a lot
is from the lodge/clubs
is from the P.T.A.
is from the children's
 sports program
would you like to do
 business with
owes you money
is in sales
has a lot of credibility
is successful
needs to make money
complains about his/her job
is from the old neighborhood
are parents of your children's
 friends
is your favorite grocery
 checker

Who is your . . .

mailman
dentist
doctor
minister
lawyer
insurance agent
children's teacher
realtor
painter
mover
night-school
 instructor
banker
florist
babysitters
babysitters parents
pharmacist
veterinarian
optometrist
dry cleaner
photographer
hair stylists
handyman
friends
neighbors
travel agent
accountant
exterminator
UPS/FedEx driver
shoe repairman
gardener
milkman

Who are your relatives . . .

parents
grandparents
sisters/brothers
cousins
aunts/uncles
stepparents
stepgrandparents
stepbrothers/sisters
former spouse
former in-laws
grandchildren
nieces/nephews

Who sold us our . . .

appliances
Avon products
bicycle
carpet
cars
cleaning products
clothes/shoes
furniture
lawn equipment
maintenance lease
lawn equipment
maintenance lease
office supplies
printing supplies
Tupperware

WORKSHEET - B

Form for "Contact List" Information

#	*Who do I know?* **Create a list of 100** **Do not prejudge**		
	Name	Phone	Comments/Relationship
1			
2			
3			
4			
5			
6			
7			
8			
9			
10			
11			
12			
13			
14			
15			
16			
17			
18			
19			
20			
21			
22			
23			
24			
25			

WORKSHEET - C

Sharing your Business and Products with Prospects

THE "INVITING CALL."

The intent of this phone call is to invite a prospect to one of your company's meetings or to make an appointment with him. What you say, of course, will vary greatly depending on how well you know the individual and what kind of relationship you have with him. Listed below are some sample opening lines that should help you get started with the very important task of "inviting."

- "I want to tell you about a business I've discovered."
- "I want to get your opinion on something that I'm involved with."
- "I've got something I want to show you."
- "Would you do me a favor?"
- "I need to discuss something with you."
- "I know you've always talked about doing something else."
- "If the right opportunity came up, would you be available?"
- "Do you know anyone who would be interested in having a business of his own?"
- "We haven't talked in a long time."
- "Are you satisfied with what you're doing right now?"
- "Are you making all the money you need?"
- "Do you think your job is secure for the future?"

WAYS TO SHARE YOUR COMPANY'S "OPPORTUNITY."

There are many different ways to share your business and its products with a prospect. Some of the most often used are listed below:

- **1 ON 1.** This is when you meet with a prospect personally and privately.
- **2 ON 1.** This is when you and your sponsor (or some other upline associate) meet with a prospect.
- **SMALL GROUP MEETING.** This is when your sponsor (or another leader) comes to your home or some other location to make a presentation to a small group of your prospects.
- **VIDEO PRESENTATION.** This is when you show your company's video presentation to one or more prospects in your home or at another location.
- Audio Presentation. This is when you play your company's audio presentation for one or more prospects.
- **LOCAL MEETING OR LUNCHEON.** This is when one or more sponsors have a meeting to share the business and its products with prospects and/or to train new sales reps.
- **LOCAL OR REGIONAL TRAINING SYMPOSIUM.** This is when leaders from the company present instructional sessions on your company's business opportunity.
- **REGIONAL PROMOTIONAL MEETING.** This is when leaders present your company's "Success Story" to recruit new people.

Note of Acknowledgment

*The authors want to thank **Claude W. Savage** and **Jeffrey Hooks** for their substantial contribution to this chapter. The content and structure of the material you have just read reflects their experience in and ideas about network marketing. Both men have impressive entrepreneurial and business backgrounds, but the biographical information below documents the credibility which these two individuals have earned in the arena of network marketing.*

***Claude W. Savage** became involved with network marketing in 1989 and achieved the highest level of sales production in his first year in the industry. He has built sales organizations which number in the 1000's, has trained hundreds of individuals who have become highly successful network marketers, and has created downline organizations that have produced $400 million a year in sales.*

***Jeffrey Hooks**, in just three years in network marketing, has developed a sales organization of over 500 distributors working in 26 states and has demonstrated that he has a strong ability for recruiting and developing a highly productive downline organization.*

3

BUILDING A RETAIL
SALES ORGANIZATION

Introduction

In the previous chapter we discussed the **"9 Steps to Success"** for an Independent Retail Sales Representative in the network marketing industry. Now we are ready to discover that the "9 Steps" can be talked about by sorting them into **"4 Categories."** Here they are!

    I.   **Study** the opportunity and **Sign** on.
    II. **Prepare** and **Plan** for success.
    III. **Commit** to the business.
    IV. **Work** for success.

Now let's place each of the "9 Steps" under the category where it belongs.

    I.   **Study** the opportunity and **Sign** on.
        1.   Study your prospective company's *Career Kit.*
        2.   Sign and mail in the *Sales Representative Agreement*
    II. **Prepare** and **Plan** for success.
        3.   Develop *Contact List.*
        4.   Develop strong belief-level...
            a.   in the industry
            b.   in your company
            c.   in yourself
        5.   Put goals on paper.
    III. **Commit** to the business.
        6.   Commit for one year.
    IV. **Work** for rewards.
        7.   Recognize and use "tools" of the business.
        8.   Maintain consistent focused activity.
        9.   Create leadership.

To summarize the "**4 Categories**" as briefly as possible, we can say:

I. **Study** and **Sign.**
II. **Prepare** and **Plan.**
III. **Commit.**
IV. **Work.**

Now let's take the first letter of each category - **S P C W** - and make an acronym that you can use every day as you share your company's story with your friends and neighbors and business associates: **S P C W = SO PEOPLE CAN WIN !!!**

After all, that's what network marketing is all about - helping people win - helping people achieve their personal and business goals so that they can improve their quality of life.

In this chapter we are going to take a detailed look at **what should happen for a new sales rep** during his **first 5 weeks** in network marketing. By the end of this time-period the new rep should have established his **own Retail Sale Organization**.

Before You Sign On

For several days (or perhaps weeks) you have been talking with a sponsor (or sponsoring representative) from your prospective company about the business. Then you attend a Business (or "Business Opportunity") Meeting held by the sponsor. You go to the meeting with a few remaining questions that have been holding you back, but get satisfactory answers to them and decide to sign on with the company.

Day 1 - Being Sponsored into the Business

Your sponsor helps you complete the company's *Sales Representative Application*, and in so doing accepts the responsibility for training you and helping you establish your own Retail Sales Organization. He will be eager to do this because his success depends upon yours. In training you, he will be **duplicating** the teaching procedure by which **he** was trained. And in helping you establish your own Retail Sales Organization, he will be **adding on** to his own. It is absolutely essential that this basic training procedure be kept simple. Only if it is kept simple will new reps be able to duplicate it for the individuals whom **they** recruit. One of the watchwords of veteran network marketers is "**Keep it simple!**"

Remember our motto - **So People Can Win**. Only if we keep our training procedure **simple** and **duplicable** will we be able to move forward and grow, and win for ourselves, for those who sponsored us, and for the countless newcomers who will join our ranks in the days and months and years of the future.

You have filled out the necessary paperwork for your sponsor, and you have ordered your company's *Career Kit* (hopefully, by "2nd Day Air" or faster). Now you must be careful **not** to do anything more regarding your new business until your *Kit* arrives. **Don't** go out and try to sell products. **Don't** attempt to recruit anyone for your own sales organization. **Don't** talk with anyone (other than your sponsor) about your business. Why not? Because you are **not ready**!

If you "hit the ground running" before you are prepared for the race, you are certain to be asked questions that you are not ready to answer. And if you are caught flat-footed, so to speak, you may fall victim to the skepticism or cynicism of a naysayer or "Dream Stealer." The world is filled with individuals who can't stand to see other people excited and upbeat about what they are doing, so don't put your dream at risk - "Don't throw your pearls to the swine" until you have made yourself strong with knowledge and are **ready** to tell the world about your new business and **defend** it against all skeptics and wiseacres. Instead, relax; rejoice in the great decision you have made, and wait for your *Career Kit* to arrive. When it does, **don't** open it. Call your sponsor immediately and make an appointment to have him walk you through it.

Week 1 - Learning the Business and Developing an Action Plan

By the end of your first week in the business you should be sitting down with your sponsor to talk about the extremely important information to be found in the *Career Kit*. He should open the box, get rid of all the packing, and completely assemble all of the materials on a table or desk for you to examine. He should tell you at the outset how important and valuable the company's *Career Kit* will be for you. Each network marketing company has its own selection of materials that are included in the new rep's start-up package (*Career Kit*), but most companies will have items such as the ones listed below. Your sponsor will walk you through them.

1. ROAD MAP TO SUCCESS. A general overview of the "steps to success" required of the network marketing sales rep.

2. QUICK-START TRAINING MANUAL.. A more detailed "nuts and bolts" discussion of the things that a new rep must do in his first 5-6 weeks with his company.

3. GOAL PLANNER. A structure for you to use in thinking about and deciding on your initial goals as a network marketing representative. You should discuss in detail with your sponsor your reasons for becoming a network marketing rep and the goals you hope to achieve with your new business. Your goals might include some of the following:

- To own a business and control your own destiny
- To pay off credit card debt
- To buy a car or house
- To make an additional few thousand dollars a month
- To meet new people and share life experiences with them
- To get away from a routine and boring pattern of living
- To put some fun and excitement into your life

It is very important for your sponsor to help you discover and articulate your goals and the motivation behind them. You should come up with short, medium and long-range goals and write them down in the *Goal Planner*. You should also write down the reason why you have set these goals. For example, if you want to earn an additional $2,000 a month so that you can build a college fund for your child, write that goal and the reason behind it down in your *Goal Planner*. Putting your goals on paper will help you stay focused for the medium and long-term. Sharing them with your sponsor will enable him to understand **what** you want to do and **why** you want to do it, and he will then be better able to help you achieve your goals. Remember, your succeeding in your new business is as important to your sponsor as it is to you.

4. BUSINESS ACTIVITY PLANNER. This is an aid to the planning and scheduling of your various business activities. The sales rep who is well organized and who plans ahead, always having a schedule that reaches several days (and even weeks) into the future) is virtually certain to succeed in network marketing. But few new reps will be able to automatically organize and schedule their activity effectively. It is your sponsor's responsibility to help you develop a Business Plan (or Action Plan) and write it into the *Business Activity Planner*. You will need to decide how many hours per week you will work your new business and then enter those hours into your *Business Activity Planner*. Your sponsor should write into your *Business Activity Planner* the dates, times, and places of all upcoming Business Briefings. All weekly meetings, 2-on-1's, 3-on-1's (see previous chapter), and various other meetings aimed at helping sales reps build successful Retail Business Organizations should be written into the *Business Activity Planner*.

It is extremely important for your sponsor to teach you to use your *Business Activity Planner* as a tool for keeping yourself organized and as a vehicle for developing a "schedule for success." He should periodically review it to be sure that you are using it productively. The sales rep who uses his *Business Activity*

Planner correctly and consistently is very likely to find his business growing by leaps and bounds.

5. INDEX FOR PROSPECTS AND CONTACTS. This is a business tool designed to help you organize information about prospects and contacts. The *Index* will enable you to organize the information which you obtain about individuals that you want to recruit for your sales organization or to whom you want to sell your company's products. In the previous chapter you discovered that there are many ways to build a prospect/contact list. By using the "Who Do You Know?" worksheet presented there you can develop a 100-name list which your sponsor can help you sort, dividing the names into the two categories of "prospects" and "contacts."

The "Prospects" section of your *Index* is for the names of and information about persons that you want to recruit for your sales organization. The "Contacts" section of the *Index* is for the names of and information about individuals to whom you want to sell products (the retail side of your business). Your sponsor should show you how to use the *Index* to record information about these two groups of people.

By this point in your meeting with your sponsor you should have developed (with his help) a Business Plan by using your *Goal Planner*, *Business Activity Planner*, and *Index for Prospects and Contacts*. These items in your company's start-up kit have now become business tools for you. You will be able to use them from now on in ways that will provide you with focus and direction for working your new business.

6. BUSINESS OPPORTUNITY BROCHURE
   PRODUCT CATALOG

Your sponsor should spend a few minutes with you explaining how these and other marketing materials in the *Career Kit* can be used effectively with prospects and contacts. While walking you through these materials, he should use the opportunity to remind you of the reason(s) you decided to build your own network marketing business.

7. BUSINESS CARD ORDER FORM

Your sponsor should help you fill out this form. He shouldn't have to explain its importance. If you are going to be in business, you need business cards.

8. BUSINESS OPPORTUNITY PRESENTATION
RETAIL PRODUCT SALES PRESENTATION
SALES REPRESENTATIVE COMPENSATION PLAN

Your sponsor will spend only a few minutes taking you through these three flip-chart presentations, but he will explain to you that they are **the vehicle** for sharing your business with other people without having to create or memorize a script or standard presentation. These three presentations **are** the script and standard presentation which you should use when you present your company's business to prospects. Your sponsor cannot, at this brief meeting intended to merely introduce you to the materials in the sales rep start-up kit, turn you into an instant "pro" at making these flip-chart presentations. That will take time, but you will become very skillful at it after you have had the opportunity to sit in on a few meetings at which your sponsor or some other leader makes the presentations.

9. SALES REPRESENTATIVE'S RESOURCE BOOK

This *Resource Book* contains 3 sections:

- Your company's "Sales Representative Compensation Plan"
- Your company's "Policies and Procedures"
- Your company's "Sales Representative Agreement Letter"

Your sponsor will tell you how important the *Resource Book* is and that you should read it several times in order to be sure you fully understand it. He will explain to you that any violation on your part, intentional or unintentional, of your company's policies and procedures could result in your immediate termination with the company. You will need to sign the "Agreement Letter" found in the *Resource Book* and mail it to the home office of your company. Many companies allow you 30 days to sign and return the sales rep agreement letter and then, if they have not yet received it, put a "hold" on your products and checks until your letter is received. Also, you will need to complete the "IRS W-9 Taxpayer Identification Form" and mail it to your company's corporate office.

10. HANDBOOK FOR PROFESSIONAL SALESPERSONS

Most network marketing companies provide new sales reps with a book designed to give them training in network marketing sales. Sometimes the book also contains general (generic) instruction in sales techniques that are valuable to all salespersons regardless of the type of sales they are in. Your sponsor should explain the value of using this book as a business tool that can accelerate the growth of your new Retail Sales Organization.

11. VARIOUS BUSINESS FORMS

Your sales rep start-up kit contains several different business forms which are used by all sales reps. Some of them are used routinely while others are used only periodically. Your sponsor should call your attention to each of the forms and help you fill them out when you need to use them. You should feel free to ask for help with them as long as you feel any need for guidance in the use of these forms. It is very important that these forms be filled out correctly and mailed in a timely manner to your corporate office whenever your business activity makes their use necessary. Simple things like doing these forms in pencil rather than ink, and writing illegibly rather than printing clearly, can cost a rep time and money.

12. YOUR COMPANY'S AUDIO AND VIDEO TAPES

These tapes provide the sales rep with valuable information about his company - its business opportunity and its products. Your sponsor should underscore their importance and urge you to review them several times so that you will be able to talk comfortably and intelligently about the company you represent.

13. YOUR COMPANY'S DATA AND COMMUNICATIONS SERVICE

To be a successful sales representative you must be able to manage your business with the timely information provided by your company's data and communication service. Most network marketing companies provide services such as the following:

- **Voice mail**
- **Sales volume status information by Business Center**
- **Fax summary of your sales organization**
- **Status of existing orders**
- **Sales aid and product ordering**
- **Locally scheduled meetings (by area code)**
- **Dates of corporate "How To" seminars**

Now your sponsor has completed walking you through the materials in your company's *Career Kit*. As a result of this meeting you should have a Business Plan for developing your own Retail Business Organization. You should have goals set and business activities scheduled for at least several days, probably even a few weeks. As this session with your sponsor comes to an end, he should assign you the task of bringing your two best prospects to the company's next Business Briefing to hear a presentation of the company's business opportunity. He should also tell you that at his next meeting with you he will expect you to update him on the status of your Goals, Business Plan, and Schedule of Business Activities.

Week 2 - Sponsoring 2 People

You should be present with your two best prospects at this week's Business Briefing. You have brought **prospects** - potential company sales representatives - **not contacts**, because this meeting is designed to introduce individuals to your company's business opportunity, not to sell products. (The focus of this chapter is on building your own Retail Sales Organization, not selling your company's products.) Your sponsor should spend a few minutes with you and your two prospects before the meeting starts. He should tell you, and them, that he will have a detailed discussion with you as soon as the Business Briefing is over. The leader who presents the company's "Business Opportunity" should use company slides and company-prepared presentation material (and **nothing else**).

After the Business Briefing, you and your two prospects will meet with your sponsor to discuss the "Business Opportunity" that has just been presented. Your sponsor should help you in *closing* the prospects into the business. (Be sure to study the chapters in this book that deal with (a) handling a prospect's objections and (b) the art of closing.) If you are successful in closing your two prospects, then you and your sponsor should share with them your own stories about how you were brought into the business.

You should explain to your new recruits how **they** can each sponsor two key prospects in the **same way** that you sponsored them. You and your sponsor should stress to the new reps that the process by which they were recruited (sponsored) is absolutely **duplicable**. It was duplicated on your sponsor, on yourself, and now on them. You must convey to them that the duplicable nature of the process of *sponsoring* and *teaching to sponsor* is at the very heart of network marketing. Before you leave the meeting, you and your sponsor should set a time when you will meet with the two new reps to walk them through your company's *Career Kit* and help each of them develop a Business Plan.

This is the end of "Week 2" for you, and you have successfully duplicated yourself. Actually you have **multiplied** yourself *times (x) two (2)*. You have laid the foundation stones of your own Retail Sales Organization! If you had **not** been successful in signing up your two prospects at the conclusion of the Business Briefing, then your sponsor would have continued working with you until you **were** successful in sponsoring two prospects.

Week 3 - Becoming a Teacher

You and your sponsor meet this week with your two new reps. Your sponsor will walk them through the materials in the *Career Kit* in the same way that he did you.

You will listen to his instruction to the new reps and may even pitch in your own two cents' worth from time to time. You will see how your sponsor helps each of the new reps write down his goals and develop a Business Plan. You will observe how he also helps them plan and schedule a calendar of business activities. In a word, you will see how your sponsor does for the two new reps the **very same things** that he did for you two weeks ago.

By sitting in on your sponsor's training of your two new reps, you will learn to be the teacher yourself for the next cycle of teaching in your sales organization. Your sponsor will not have to conduct the training again in **your** sales organization. By teaching you how to duplicate the training, he frees himself to train **other** new reps that he sponsors, and in turn, **their** first-line recruits.

It is impossible to overstate the importance of the first two "rounds" of training done by a sponsor. If a sponsor does a good job of teaching his first-line recruit and then, in turn, the two new reps sponsored by that individual, the sponsor is then able to absent himself from any further training in that sales organization! That is what we mean by the process of duplication. On the other hand, if a sponsor does a poor job of training a new rep, he will find himself doomed to an endless cycle of repeating that half-baked training to new rep after new rep because he did not teach his original recruit how to duplicate the teaching process.

Week 4 - Developing as a Leader

This week you will attend a Business Briefing to which the two new reps you have just sponsored (and helped train) will each bring two prospects of their own. You will find yourself repeating the role played by **your** sponsor (with you and your two prospects....who are **now** your reps) at the Business Briefing two weeks ago. Before the meeting starts, you will talk with your two new reps and their four prospects. When the Business Briefing is over, you will meet with them again and help your reps to close their prospects into the business **just as your sponsor did with you two weeks ago**. Then you will make an appointment for next week with your reps and their four new recruits to walk the new individuals through the *Career Kit*, set goals, develop a Business Plan, schedule a calendar of business activities, etc.

The duplication process is alive and well in your new Retail Sales Organization!

Week 5 - Repeating the Cycle

You have now become a successful **sponsor** in your company, and you have two well-trained and highly motivated sales reps in your sales organization who **now** have their **own** Retail Sales Organizations (with two reps each). Most importantly, perhaps, the two reps you sponsored and trained are now prepared and motivated to help **others** become successful.

The two reps that you sponsored just 3 weeks ago have themselves now experienced the training cycle two times. **First**, they experienced it *personally*, as they were taught by your sponsor, as prospects and then as new reps. Then they experienced it a **second** time as *listeners* when you taught their prospects and then trained them as new reps. So, they have been *students* and are now ready to be *teachers*. You can wean them now, **just as your sponsor weaned you**, to take over the development of their own sales organizations. And you can move on to sponsor new prospects and help them establish their own Retail Sales Organizations.

Summary

In this chapter we have explained how as a network marketing sales representative you can build your own Retail Sales Organization. We have seen that the procedure that must be followed is both **simple** and **duplicable**. The importance of these two characteristics cannot be stressed too much. If the procedure is not simple - if it is complicated and cumbersome - it will be difficult to teach to new representatives. If the procedure is not duplicable - if new reps cannot duplicate and multiply themselves - then the single greatest benefit of network marketing is lost - an individual cannot infinitely multiply his productivity through his sales organization. But, if your company is like most network marketing companies, the procedure for building a Retail Sales Organization **is** simple and duplicable! It was **planned** that way.......... **SPCW !!! So People Can Win !!!**

INDEX

INDEX

INDEX

For additional copies of this book.....

Contact the publisher's agent:

Mayflower Holdings, Inc.
P.O. Box 30096
Raleigh, NC 27622
Phone: (919) 881-7993
Fax: (919) 881-8375

Discount Rates Available
1 - 5 Copies	=	$13.95
6 -10 Copies	=	$12.95
11 + Copies	=	$11.95

Professional Consulting Service

The authors of this book are available to do professional consulting (seminars, trouble-shooting, etc.) in the areas of Sales, Marketing, and Sales Management. Interested parties should contact them at the address above.